Choosing Your Cebuano with Collocations

STAND OUT MORE ARTICULATE

ALFONSO BORELLO

CHOOSING YOUR CEBUANO WTH COLLOCATIONS

Choosing Your Cebuano with Collocations: Stand Out More Articulate

Cover designed by Alfonso Borello

Published in the United States of America

First Printed Edition: March 2022

Includes index

ISBN: 9798422223015 (Paperback)

Contents

What is it?

The purpose of this book is accelerated learning of the Cebuano language. This learning method is an essential tool used by polyglots to increase retention. The clusters are based on frequency. The corpus of origin has more than 1 million words with 80,000+ distinct words (ENG/CEB) with emphasis on dialog, idiomatic expressions, and colloquialism from the research work of John Wolff at Cornell University/Southeast Asia Program in Ithaca, New York in 1971.

Review the index on a regular basis for better recall. It isn't ornamental, it's there for a reason. It contains concordances and the complete list of word clusters. Please note that grave and acute accents denote stress on pronunciation, and aren't generally used in writing.*

*Collocation inclusion is based on high frequency of concordance.

Sa

SIYA SA IYANG

Kas-aha (kas-ahi) ug sulti arun dì magdahum nga gastúhan siya sa íyang pagiskuyla, Tell him frankly not to count on our sending him to school.

Mipadaplin siya sa íyang gibása ug namátì sa tabì, She put aside what she was reading and listened to gossip.

Giundángan na siya sa íyang dugù, Her menstruation has stopped.

Miúmat siya sa íyang kaági sa gúbat, He related his experiences during the war.

Nagsulti siya sa íyang kaugalíngun, She was talking to herself.

Ug mupaubus siya sa íyang pusil ayaw ug tirúhi, If he lowers his gun, don't shoot him.

Mipaubus siya sa íyang tíngug, hadluk hidunggan, He lowered his voice, afraid of being heard.

Bísan pag tuwarun ninyu siya, mudukut giyud siya sa íyang diklarasiyun, No matter how well you cross-examine him he will stick to his declaration.

SA USA KA
Lima ka klási ang gibanting sa usa ka maistru, The teacher was burdened with five classes

Lagmit ang kadátù makaamyat (makapaamyat) sa usa ka asáwa, Usually wealth makes a wife think too highly of herself.

Kinahanglan sa usa ka anawunsir nga maáyu muadlib, It's necessary for an announcer to be good.

Ang pagyuhut sa usa ka mabiaybiáyung tamíhid sa íyang mga ngábil, When a smile of derision formed itself on his lips.

Madá ang rám sa usa ka yaruk, You can drink the rum in one gulp.

Nawalis (niwalis) ang íyang mga ngábil sa usa ka maanindut nga pahíyum, Her lips turned up in a sweet smile.

Miutnga siya sa pag-alsa sa usa ka sákung kupras, He grunted when he lifted the sack of copra.

Sa usa ka púlung siyay nidaug, In short, he would be a certain (unnamed) one.

Giutlan ang duha námù ka balay sa usa ka mutu, Our houses are separated by a hill.

SA IYANG MGA

Ang pagyuhut sa usa ka mabiaybiáyung tamíhid sa íyang mga ngábil, When a smile of derision formed itself on his lips.

Daw búang siya nga nagwaldaswaldas sa íyang mga kamut, He waves his arms around like a madman when he speaks.

Lúnung ko níya sa íyang mga salà, He wants to implicate me in his offenses.

Ubligasiyun sa usa ka ginikánan pagbuhì sa íyang mga anak, Parents have an obligation to raise their children.

Kanang inahána nagpatumbayà lang sa íyang mga anak, That mother is neglecting her children.

Natirbisíya siya ug karun lúgus na makabisti sa íyang mga anak, He suffered a misfortune and now he can hardly clothe his children.

Ang pag-inum-ínum ray íyang itápak sa íyang mga kaguul, He drowns his sorrows in alcohol.

Lúhà nga nanambù (mitambù) sa íyang mga mata, Tears that formed in her eyes.

Nakatagaw na siya sa íyang mga saup, He has already made the rounds of his tenants.

KO SA AKONG

Nagyangud ko sa akong magúwang sa pagiskuyla, I rely on my brother to support me in school.

Nag-unanut ko sa akong mga sabdyiks rung tuíga, I am having difficulty with my subjects this year.

Mubakasiyun ko kay magpahiulì ko sa akong láwas, I'll take a vacation to regain my health.

Muúlà ko sa akong dugù álang sa yútang natawhan, I'll shed my blood for my native land.

Manrinsas pa ko sa akong pinangkù, I'm still putting hairpins in my chignon.

Magtápak ko sa akong naabsinan, I'll make up for the time I lost when I was absent.

Natálang ko sa akong tubag kay sayup kaáyu, I was embarrassed because my answer was complete.

Nagsúli ko sa akong kábaw nga nakabuhì, I'm looking for my carabao which got loose.

Nasayup ko sa akong kalkúlu, I am wrong in my calculation.

Saplan ko sa akong tiyù sa gastu sa iskuylahan, My uncle will shoulder my school fees.

ANG BATA SA

Nagyapayapa ang bátà sa kalípay, The child waved his arms for joy.

Nagyangud ang bátà sa íyang tabánug, The boy is looking at his kite.

Miyam-id (nangyam-id) ang bátà sa pagkáun, The child pouted at the food.

Miuha ang bátà sa pagguwà, The child cried when it came out.

Mipatúud ang bátà sa íyang samad sa íyang inahan, The child showed his mother his wound.

Nanáup ang bátà sa daghang táwu, The child disappeared in the midst of the crowd.

Natambug ang bátà sa hagdanan, The child fell down the stairs.

Itambù ang bátà sa bintánà, Put the child in the window.

Akong giub-an ang bátà sa nagpungasì na ang bála, I threw myself on the child when the bullets came fast.

Mitabuylug ang bátà sa písì, The child hung to a rope and swung around.

ANG TUBIG SA

Nag-agay-ay ang túbig sa punúan sa káhuy, The water is trickling very slowly down the trunk of the tree.

Mituhuy ang túbig sa hús, The water from the hose is spurting out far.

Mutúhud na ang túbig sa dálan, The water in the street is nearly up to the knees.

Gáhì musunub ang túbig sa yútang kúnun, Water doesn't seep easily into clay soil.

Sulug kaáyu ang túbig sa subà, The water in the river is swift.

Mawálà ang lim-aw ug musuhup (masuhup) na ang túbig sa yútà, The pool will disappear when the water seeps into the ground.

Ang túbig sa mga sapà musúguk ngadtu sa dágat, The water from the streams rushes into the sea.

Misubwak ang túbig sa tuburan, The water gushed out of the source of the spring.

Misílit ang túbig sa grípu, The water flowed from the faucet.

Ang túbig sa bukána sa subà sampurádu, The mouth of a river is a mixture of salt and fresh.

SA MGA TAWU
Giyagubyúban sa mga táwu ang mamumulung, The people muttered angrily as he gave his speech.

Ang íyang hinanálì nga kamatáyun mauy nakaugnuk (nakapaugnuk) sa mga táwu, His sudden death stunned the people.

Ang bwangan mauy tambakan sa mga táwu matag Duminggu, The cockpit is where the people gather on Sundays.

Hinganlan nákù pasunud ang ngálan sa mga táwu sa laráwan gíkan sa wala ngadtu sa túu, I will name the people in the picture in order from left to right.

Ang nahitabù nahímung sultiánan sa mga táwu, What happened became a subject of conversation for the people.

Ságad sa mga táwu dinhi, Most of the people here.

Ang lawak napunù sa mga táwu, The room was filled with people.

Ang maung hitabù nahímung ginahisgútan sa mga táwu, That event became the subject of conversation for these people.

Ang linya sa mga táwu miabut ngadtu sa iskína, The queue reached to the corner.

KA SA IMUNG

'Unsa, nakagustu ka sa ímung trabáhu?', 'How do you like your work?'

Kinahanglang mutúu ka sa ímung asáwa, You have to do what your wife tells you.

Naunay ka sa ímung tinuntu, It serves you right.

Um? kusiun ta giyud ka sa ímung minalditu, Humph, I have to pinch you, you are so mischievous.

Nagkaulipun ka sa ímung bisyu, You are becoming a slave to your vices.

Mauy nakaáyu kanímu kay dì giyud ka mutukul kun buyagun ka sa ímung sayup, One thing good about you is you never nurse a grudge against people.

Nagsugal ka sa ímung kinabúhì ánang trabahúa, You are risking your life in that work.

Sigúru kang maánur ug siryúsu ka sa ímung pagtuun, You will get honors if you are serious with your studies.

Isambilay nang bag arun makahayun ka sa ímung buktun, Sling the bag over your shoulder so you can swing your arms.

SIYA SA MGA
Hubgun ko siya sa mga sáad, I will make her drunk with promises.

Nakatálì na siya sa mga putus, She has bound the packages.

Nagtágik siya sa mga nípà didtu sa katsaw, He was tying the nipa strips to the rafters.

Usa siya sa mga tinagad nga táwu sa lungsud, He is one of the respected people in the town.

Nasugmaw siya sa mga útang, She plunged herself into debt.

Nagsánib siya sa mga papil, She is stacking the papers in a neat pile.

Nagpintul siya sa mga sugnud, He is cutting the firewood into lengths.

Munikinikinu siya sa mga babáye, He teases the women.

Gimirun nà siya sa mga tahur, The professional gamblers use him to help place their bets.

KO SA IYANG
Nahiubus ko sa íyang sulti, I was hurt by what he said.

Natingála ko sa íyang pagkausab, It surprised me at how he had changed.

Napikal ko sa íyang matamihírun nga katáwa, I got irked at her derisive laughter.

Gisumhan ko sa íyang pangatarúngan, I was bored with his reasoning.

Nahasinta ko sa íyang tinubagan, I was taken aback by the way he talked back.

Gipul-an ko sa íyang mga isturya, I'm bored with her stories.

Magsingil na ko sa íyang gibúhat nákù, I will now collect for what he has done to me.

Nakasiklit ko sa íyang gisulat, I got a glimpse of what he wrote.

Nakasaway ko sa íyang gisulti sa íyang diskursu, I think it's improper what he said in his speech.

Satispitsu ko sa íyang ági, I'm satisfied with his work.

Giputian (gipaputian) ko siyag sulti nga naglágut ko sa íyang gibúhat, I had it out with her because I was angry at what she did.

Hilagputan ko sa íyang láway, I was hit by his spit.

Nakalabak ko sa íyang samput, I spanked her on the buttocks.

Gikundátan kaáyu ko sa íyang sinayawan, I consider her way of dancing boisterous and unbecoming.

Nakapanahì ko kay nakakarahay (nakapangarahay) man ko sa íyang makina, I managed to sew some things because I got to use her sewing machine.

Mitigkáhuy ko sa íyang tinápuk, I gathered the wood he had piled up.

Íbug ko sa íyang sinínà, I am very much attracted to her dress.

Gihilásan ko sa íyang hambug, I find it revolting the way he brags.

NA KO SA

Nakatungà na ko sa libru, I'm halfway through the book.

Talilarga na ko sa Amirika, I'm ready to leave for America.

Nagtakamtakam na ko sa lamì sa mga sud-an, I am eagerly anticipating the delicious food.

Nasáyud na ko sa ímung tinagúan, I know your secret.

Naswítu na ko sa inyung sikrítu, I have found out your secret.

Súmad niá run túa na ko sa Amirika, A year from now I will be in America.

Magsípung na ko sa kálù, I'll finish weaving the outer edges of the brim of the hat.

Magsingil na ko sa íyang gibúhat nákù, I will now collect for what he has done to me.

Nakapalag (nakahipálag) na ko sa hustung tubag, I found the right answer.

Mau ra ug nahuwasan na ko sa akong kakulbà, I feel a bit relieved from my fright.

SA DI PA

Mag-ílis úsà ko sa dì pa ta manglákaw, I'll change my clothes first before we go out.

Idalì ang bátà sa huspital sa dílì pa tupayun, Bring the child at once to the hospital before it becomes uncoscious.

Magsiyatsíyat únà ang mga magduduwà sa dì pa sugdan ang baskit, The players do practice shooting before the game starts.

Manlukluk ta sa dì pa magpayring, Let's get out of the way before the firing starts.

Natigúlang ko sa dì pa sa akong panáhun, I became an old man before my time.

Ságad pagabasáhun níya ang Biblíya sa dì pa matúlug, She usually reads the Bible before she goes to sleep.

Hipúsa ang libru sa dílì pa si Pápa muabut, Put the book away before Dad arrives.

Lima na lang ka minútu sa dílì pa ang alas singku, It is five minutes before five o'clock.

Manggáwas ta sa dì pa mulundag ang barku, Let's go over the side before the boat sinks.

SA PANAHUN SA
Ang suburnu nabúhat sa panahun sa prisidinti pa si Makapagal, The bribery was done when Macapagal was president.

Sa panahun sa girilya ang ámung nutisya gíkan sa radiyu balágun (kawáyan), During the war we got our news over the grapevine.

Sa panahun sa libirasiyun, In the liberation period.

Ang kábaw sa panahun sa ting-init mulígid sa tunaan, On hot days the carabao wallows in the pond.

Daghang gikuraw sa panahun sa gúbat, Many people died of starvation during the war.

Mukalàkalà giyud ang mga bakì sa panahun sa ting-ulan, Frogs croak on rainy days.

Ang Munlayit Sirinid sunghit sa panahun sa gíra, 'Moonlight Serenade' was popular during the war.

Naggirilya ang mga kalakin-an sa panahun sa ukupasiyun, The men became guerillas during the Japanese occupation.

Kanà si Ámuy Militun kapitan sa panahun sa Katsílà, Amoy Meliton was a village head during the Spanish times.

Ug

UG DI KA
Balaun (ibalà) tikaw sa klási ug dì ka magtuun, I'll fail you if you don't study.

Ug dì ka muubù masungkù ka, If you don't stoop, you'll bump your head.

Ang manuk nakatuklù ug duha ka bakì, The chicken has caught two frogs pecking at them.

Ug dílì ka mutugan, kastigúhun ka, If you don't confess, I will beat you.

Magtangsà (matangsà) ka giyud ug dì ka mukáug maáyu, You'll grow thin if you don't eat well.

Surupun (surupan) ka ug dì ka maghábul nga matúlug, You will have gas pains if you sleep without cover.

Masunda giyud ka ug dì ka makaihì, You'll be catheterized if you can't urinate.

Akuy musugba sa ímung duláan ug dì ka maghílum, I will throw your toys into the fire if you aren't quiet.

Siwángun tikaw run ug dì ka magtárung, I'll split your lips open if you don't behave.

UG USA KA

Miútang (nangútang) ko ug usa ka gantang bugas, I bought a ganta of rice on credit.

Gipauwanuwánan mi sa kandidátu ug usa ka kahun nga sirbísa, The candidate treated us to a case of beer.

Ang dálan mitúlin ug usa ka kilumitru ubay sa subà, The path ran for a kilometer along the river.

Mutimbang ug usa ka tuniláda, It weighs one ton.

Kanang grupúha mutumba ug usa ka tárung tubà, That group will consume one kerosene can of palm toddy.

Si Hárì Artur gitugáhan ug usa ka ispáda, King Arthur was given a sword by a supernatural being.

Nagkinahanglan pa ta ug usa ka táyun nga túbu, We still need a length of water pipe.

Gitasalan ang masakitun sa kansir ug usa ka búlan, The cancer patient was given a month to live.

Gitampáan siya ug usa ka balay ug usa ka lunà nga yútà, They paid a house and a piece of land for it.

Mutágud ning basáka ug usa ka bákid, This rice field is big enough to have one cavan planted on it.

UG MAAYU ANG

Muális ug maáyu ang ispidbut ug pakusgan, The speedboat produces high waves in its wake when it runs fast.

Nag-ukpaw-ukpaw ug maáyu ang kabáyù, The horse was galloping wildly.

Itakam (takama) ug maáyu ang kan-un únà tunla, Chew the food well before you swallow it.

Pugaa (pug-a) ug maáyu ang limunsítu, Squeeze the calamondin dry.

Pakgúti ug maáyu ang kahoy, Tie the firewood together securely.

Ibaklíad (bakliára) ug maáyu ang ímung láwas, Bend your body far back.

Pigisa (pigsa, ipigis) ug maáyu ang kakaw, Crush the cacao fine.

UG WA KAY

Way tugalbung – tugdan mutúgal (manúgal) ug wà kay útang, Nobody disturbs you if you don't have any debts.

Puul kaáyu ning kinabúhì ug wà kay lingawlingaw, Life is very boring if you have no leisure.

Mumirma ang ímung láwas ug wà kay tulug, You will lose weight if you lack sleep.

Ug wà kay lingaw, pagtuun, If you don't have anything to do, you could study.

Lisud ang pangimplíyu ug wà kay alam, You'll have a hard time finding a job if you have no education.

Mauntup ang ímung tubag ug wà kay láing ikasulti, Your answer will be short if you have nothing else to say.

Ayawg kíha ug wà kay kamatuúran, Don't sue if you have no proof.

Kay

KAY WA KUY

Makalakaw ko bísan ása kay wà kuy gabing, I can go out anywhere because there is no one I have to stay with.

Dílì ko makasígi karung sunod túig kay wà kuy kwarta, I cannot proceed with my studies next year because I have no money.

Mamursiyintu lang ko kay wà kuy láing karimidiyúhan, I'll borrow money because I have no other place to stay.

Muplíti ra kug libru kay wà kuy ipalit, I'll just rent my books because I don't have enough money to buy them.

Pit-us kaáyu mi kay wà kuy trabáhu, We're very hard up because I don't have a job.

Napangkàpangkà ko kay wà kuy trabáhu, I was in desperate financial straits because I had no job.

Ayaw pangáyù nákù kay wà kuy nahut, Don't ask me for anything because I'm penniless.

Naglisuay (nagkalisuay) ko íning trabáhu kay wà kuy katábang, I'm up to my neck with work because I don't have anybody to help me.

KAY WA MAN

Nagtunguptúngup lang ko sa úras kay wà man kuy rilu, I'm just estimating the time because I don't have a watch.

Gitsíhan lang ko níya kay wà man kuy barku, She just snorted at me because I'm not rich.

Magpayà mi sa ámù kay wà man miy plátu, We use coconut shell plates because we don't have dishes.

Dì ka mutagad nákù kay wà man kuy náda nímu, You don't notice me because I am nothing to you.

Namatay ang tanum kay wà man gud bùbúi, The plant died because no one watered it.

Akuy milangkap sa íyang bayranan kay wà man siyay kwarta, I paid up all her obligations because she had no money.

Maggútus na lang ta kay wà man giyuy sakyanan, We have to walk because there's no transportation.

Dan, kay walà man siya mutuun, nahagbung, So, since he didn't study, he failed.

Wà makahimúsak (makapanghimúsak) ang humay kay wà man abunúhi, The rice did not bear in abundance because it wasn't fertilized.

KAY WA PA

Dì sà mi muúlì sa ámung lisinsiya kay wà pa miy babáye, We won't stop having babies until we have a girl.

Kambásun (kambásan) nátù sila kay wà pa sila hibaligyai, Let's canvass them because they haven't bought any.

Ayawg kahangyi nà kay wà pa mahuman, Don't dare touch that because it's not done.

Iríhis pa ni si Nituy kay wà pa kasimba, Nitoy is still a heretic because he hasn't gone to church yet.

KAY WA NA

Mag-uruyúruy ta kay wà na tay ginikánan, Let us go easy on each other because we don't have parents.

Urálun ta na lang ning sinugbang isdà kay walà na may kan-un, Let's just eat the broiled fish alone because there's no food.

Magpasagad lang ko dinhi kay wà na kuy mga paryinti, I'll stay here to rot for I have no more family.

Lisdan ko magkinatsilà kay wà na kuy praktis, I have a hard time speaking Spanish because I don't have practice.

Kayátun ko siya run kay wà na dug-a, I'll have her today because she's not menstruating any more.

Nag-istanding kung nagkaun kay walà na may lingkuránan, I ate standing because there were no more seats.

Íla na lang ko nga isingisingun (iising-ising) kay wà na man kuy kapuslánan, They'll avoid me now, for I'm no longer of any use.

Indispír ko kay wà na kuy huwaman, I'm desperate because I don't know who to borrow from.

Giapuyáhan na ko ning nilugáwa kay wà na may lanut, This porridge is all pulp because there is no water.

LANG TA KAY

Magtsík lang ta kay wà nay láin, Let's just share this cigarette because I haven't got any more.

Managaytay lang ta kay gibahaan ang ubus, Let's travel along the ridge because the valleys are flooded.

Maglinata lang ta kay kápuy ilútù, Let's just have canned foods because I'm too lazy to cook.

Maghinayhínay na lang ta kay hápun na man, Let's get going because it's late.

KAY WAY KAY

Ayawg patugatuga ug pangulitáwung Maríya kay wà kay subu, Don't try to court Mary because you are inexperienced.

Bakákun ka kay wà kay púlung, You're a liar because you didn't keep your word.

Ayg tak-in kay wà kay lubut, Don't tuck in your shirt because you have flat buttocks.

Ayaw ug uban námù kay wà kay lisinsiya ni Pápa, Don't go with us because you don't have Daddy's permission.

KAY HAPIT NA

Buhíi ang klási kay hápit na mutayim (matayim), Dismiss the class because it's almost time.

Tabanga siya kay hápit na malumus, Rescue him because he's drowning.

Pugapugáha (pugapugáhi) ninyug hípus ang binulad kay hápit na muulan, Gather the rice quick because it is about to rain.

Kabang ang íyang tíngug kay hápit na maulitáwu, His voice is uneven because he is an adolescent.

Naghanut siya kay hápit na mamatay, He was gasping because he was about to die.

Exercise

Fill in the missing word: *sa, ug, or kay.*

Magsalud tas gábà musúkul ta átung ginikánan, We will earn heaven's wrath if we defy our parents.

Ayaw pagunauna sabákun tikawg dráyib, Don't try to drive on your own.

Nangúrug ang akong kaunuran kalágut, My flesh trembled in anger.

Hidakan giyud ko mikaniku dì nákù rimurimúhun ning akong dyíp, The mechanic is going to charge me too for my jeep.

Wà makarili ang awutpus urdir, The outpost did not relay the order.

Nagrapid páyir kug panglimpyu mulakaw ko, I'm cleaning the house rapidly because I'm going out.

Ang bugtung anak mauy nakapuphu pagkabutangs tigúlang, The only son inherited the old man's estate.

Ilung ray gadakù ánang putúta pungkù kaáyu, Everything is diminutive in that midget except his squat nose.

Nagpulsu ang akong dungandúngan kasakit, My temple is throbbing with pain.

Pilit brík ang íyang awtu, His car's brakes function efficiently.

Ayawg dulái nà makapildi ka, wà ibáyad, Don't play with that because you have no money.

Human na mang iksámin, dì magpasyandu dulur magpakítà balur, The examination is over so now I can just stroll about.

Ígù lang mamínaw kadiyut sakit kining akong tambal, This medicine just gives me temporary relief.

mapaburabli ang hángin sayu tang muabut píkas isla, If the wind is favorable we'll get to the other island quickly.

Paburabli kaáyu ko ímung mga plánu, I'm very favorable to your plans.

Dinumiru ang ílang pagtawag ílang mga binatunan, They call their servants by shouting out a number.

Magmidiya lútu ko human tulu ka búlan pagkamatay akong amahan, I'll go out of full mourning three months after my father's death.

Aku ray mumanumánu akong balay, I'll build my house by myself.

Gimanumánu (gimanumanúhan) lang námù ning pagpanghulma halu blak, We are molding the hollow blocks by hand.

Ayawg kanáug sílung náay mámaw, Don't go out because there is a bogeyman.

Nagmakinilya siya písì angkla, He is winding the anchor line around the windlass.

Nagmaagmaag ang diskursu pulitiku, The politician is talking incoherently.

Lupug siya bag-u pang naáyu, He is weak because he just recovered from an illness.

Milupad (gilúpad) ang akong ispiritu íyang dakung tíngug, I was terribly frightened by his loud voice.

Túa na lang giyud maglublub si Lusyu íyang badyikdyik, Lucio has finally gone to live with his woman.

Gwápa ang milaw-it lukung búlak íyang líug, A beautiful lady hung a garland around his neck.

Lampákun (ilampak) hángin ang kawáyan, The wind bends and cracks the bamboo tree.

Bisag way gilagut mutan-aw giyud sini, Even when there is no money for food, she has to go to the show.

Ámung gikuntra risibúhan ang dukumintu pálit, We have executed a document nullifying the sale.

Akong kunsirbahun (kunsirbarun, ikunsirb?r) ang mga karáang mga butang akong mga apuhan, I'll save the old things which belong to my grandparents.

Túa pa kumpisálan, She's still out back.

Ayawg ikiwatkíwat nang rúlir hikiwatan ta, Don't wave the ruler around.

Manginhas ta mukighud ang taúbun, We will gather shells when the tide begins to ebb.

Kas-aha (kas-ahi) sulti arun dì magdahum nga gastúhan siya íyang pagiskuyla, Tell him frankly not to count on our sending him to school.

Mga kanyun nga nagkanugkug pagbumbardíyu baybay, Thundering cannons shelling the shore.

Ang gikantar papílis mau nga akuy tag-íya yútà, The document states that I am the owner of the land.

Nikaman atinsiyun ang sarhintu, The sergeant gave the command of attention.

Nakamagung na ka pagkinalígù dágat, You have become dark because you always bathe in the sea.

Kadastrálun (ikadastral) ang tanang yútà búkid, All the lands on the mountain will be surveyed for tax purposes.

Isplitun (iisplit) ang klási dakù ra, The class is split if it is too big.

Ang way pagsinabtanay mauy nakaisplit partídu, Lack of mutual understanding split the party.

Nag-una ka ra tayming, You didn't come in right.

Nag-ingkargu na kug mga dapat balay, I have ordered the things we need to build the house.

Nag-ilik mig mga upisyal ámung klási, We elected our class officers.

Trabahanti nga walà muilag ulag ínit paghuman taytáyan, Workers that didn't mind the rain and heat in building the bridge.

Ang íhì labud makapásù kunu, They say millepede excretions burn the skin.

Mihútuy ang íyang buktun nga nayab-an ínit túbig, She developed a big red blister on her arm when she spilled hot water.

Muhuswà lang ílang higdaánan inigmata, These children are like hermit crabs.

Hubashúbas ning panápì sugarul, For gamblers, money comes and goes at irregular intervals.

Barátu ang mangga karun naghíya pagbúnga, Mangoes are cheap because they are fruiting in vast quantity.

Wà pa ko níya hitsúi báyad, He has not paid me in full.

Hitsúa ang usa ka búhat úsà ka magsúgud láing buluhatun, Finish one piece of work before you start s.t. else.

Hawnga tung káyu maglung-ag na ta, Rekindle the fire because we are going to cook rice now.

Pulis ang nagháras mga pumipilì, The police harassed the voters.

Muhapnut ang sikwáti ayúhun kusukúsu, Chocolate becomes smooth and thick if it is well stirred.

Makaigù langgam nga maglupad, He is a good shot.

Hamilsing ang bátà nga pinainum gátas, A child who is fed with milk is healthy.

Hamilsing ang mga tanum walug, The plants in the valley are healthy.

Mag-ugnap ang hubag nga maghakut nánà, A boil develops a throbbing pain when it begins to accumulate pus.

Mugutì (magutì) ang inyung kapital sigíhag útang, You're going to run out of capital if you keep extending credit.

Dì pa makagíwaw ang turuk pugas humay duha ka adlaw, In two days the rice sprouts still won't have come out.

Migíwaw na ang adlaw pagmata nákù, The sun had started to appear when I woke up.

May gats ka makawan tu tri kas Wayt Guld, You have got to have guts to steal s.t. at the White Guild.

Garisun giyud ka magsígi kag táak lápuk, You'll get scabies if you keep wading in the mud.

Wà siya makagangù sanga, He was not able to break the branch off.

Migangù ang tiil lamísa, The leg of the table broke off.

Makalalakaw ko bísan ása wà kuy gabing, I can go out anywhere because there is no one I have to stay with.

Dulurúsag dagway gibulagan trátu, She has a sad look because her boy friend left her.

Na

NA ANG MGA

Ug matuay na ang mga mais, aníhun na nátù, If the corn is quite bent over, we can harvest it.

Misiping (naniping) na ang mga sibúyas, The onions are multiplying.

Nasálup na ang adlaw ug namátug na ang mga manuk, The sun has set and the chickens have gone to roost.

Naputaputa na ang mga papílis sa kaban, The papers in the trunk are all brittle with age.

Nagkapusgay na ang mga simintu sa dáyik, The cement on the dike is slowly crumbling.

Pripábun (iprípab) na ang mga bagung iskuylahan karun, The schools are all going to be prefabs.

Nagkalingkús na ang mga dáhun sa tabákù nga naláyà na, The tobacco leaves are curling up now that they are withering.

Gikuyawkuyáwan na ang mga kandidatu, Election is near and the candidates are now becoming troubled.

NA LANG ANG

Mga libakíra nga dagkù, nanipis na lang ang mga wait, They are a bunch of gossips with their thin lips.

Sa kaapíki sa mga buluhatun sa panimalay naumnis na lang ang akong paniudtu, I was so busy with the housework that I missed my meal.

Sag-ulúhun ko na lang ang paniudtu, I'll just skip lunch.

Ulahia (iulahi) na lang ang uban nga dì na madala, Just leave those things you cannot take along behind.

Gastúha na lang ang ímung tinagúan, Just spend your savings.

Pipila na lang ang nahibilin, Only a few are left. Píla n queue.

Piláhay na lang ang nanghibilin sa ámung buungun, Only a few of our pomelos are left.

Napáaw ang amahan kay diyútay na lang ang bugas, The father got worried because there was little rice left.

Ilùlù na lang ang ímung kahígal, Just masturbate your craving away.

Sukad sila namalhin aku na lang ang nahibilin, After they moved away I was the only one left.

NA GANI ANG

Maupisyal na gánì ang ímung apuwintmint, Once your appointment becomes official.

Mag-ungaw na gánì ang akong kwarta sa kahurutun, mukáun na lang ko ug buwad, When my money is nearly gone I resort to eating dried fish.

Mutuktugáuk na gánì ang mga manuk, sa átù pa duul na ang kabuntágun, When the cock crows, we know morning is near.

Matíma na gánì ang trabáhu, When the work is done.

Nagtiliskupyu na gánì ang uban, The people are eating in full swing now.

Mupwirsa (mapwirsa, mamwirsa) na gánì ang ulan, mubahà giyud, If the rain pours down hard it is likely to flood.

Mapusgay na gánì ang kristal, dì na maúlì, Once the glass is shattered, it can't be repaired.

Muhimúsak (muhimusak) na gánì ang ulan, malígù ko, If the rain falls in torrents I'll bathe in it.

Mupasádu (mapasádu) na gánì ang sardínas, ilábay na lang, If the can of sardines is already spoiled, throw it away.

NA KAAYU ANG

Klús na kaáayu ang managtrátu, The lovers are now very intimate.

Ukupádu na kaáyu ang átung sakyanan, Our bus is already full.

Uga na kaáyu ang kupras, The copra is very dry now.

Tulug na kaáyu ang bátà, The child is sound asleep.

Suud na kaáyu ang adlaw sa kasal, The wedding day is near.

Siryus na kaáyu ang masakitun, The patient is very serious.

Sanguwal na kaáyu ang sinultihan sa nagpinal, The dying man's speech is very unclear now.

Lúya na kaáyu ang himatyun níyang inahan, His dying mother is already very weak.

Mahal na kaáyu ang bugas karun, Rice is very expensive now.

Húmuk na kaáyu ang kapáyas kay latung na man, The papaya has turned soft because it is very ripe.

Nakundatan na kaáyu ang ámung míd, Our maid has become flirtatious now.

KA NA SA

Nangulílang ka na sa paniudtu, You are late for dinner.

Tipik ka na sa akong kaugalíngun, You're already a part of my being.

Sa ríng dì ka makatayim ug kupúgan ka na sa kuntra, In the ring you can't ask for time-out when your opponent mauls you.

Gisulában ka na sa pagtabakù sa upyum, You are already addicted to smoking opium.

Namuaypúay ka na sa katambuk, You're bursting at the seams, you're so fat.

Makabalik ka na sa trabáhu kay nakaligù (nakakaligù) na ka, You may go back to work because you are all better now.

Lisud ka nang maminyù ug mulápas (malápas) ka na sa kalindaryu, You'll find it hard to get married if you get above thirty.

Ug magminyù ka, may kuydáwu ka na sa kinabúhì, If you marry, you have responsibilities on you.

Karun nga may kumprumísu ka na sa ímung kinabúhì, pagbinuutan na, Now that you're married, you must resolve to be good.

NA ANG ADLAW
Migíwaw na ang adlaw sa pagmata nákù, The sun had started to appear when I woke up.

Nagkatúnud (nagkatunud) na ang adlaw sa kasadpan, The sun is sinking in the west.

Alas dúsi na kay tuktuk na ang adlaw, It is twelve noon because the sun is at its zenith.

Mingitngit ang kalibútan dihang nakatik-up na ang adlaw, The earth became dark after the sun had set.

Misil-it na ang adlaw sa akong pagmata, The sun had already started to rise when I woke up.

Misiang na ang adlaw, The sun is partly out now.

Nasálup na ang adlaw ug namátug na ang mga manuk, The sun has set and the chickens have gone to roost.

Sa nagsalum na ang adlaw, As the sun was setting.

Milubug na ang adlaw sa kasadpan, The sun was about to set.

Palandúngi (palandungi) ang kábaw kay ínit na ang adlaw, Put the carabao in the shade because the sun is hot now.

NA SAD ANG

Nautas na sad ang masakitun, The sick man became unconscious again.

Giunuran na sad ang íyang láwas, He has gotten flesh back on his body.

Nía na sad ang kuníhu, karun pa magpakítà, Here you are, you s.o.b.

Nagkakaransa na sad ang magtiáyung palaaway, The quarrelsome couple is at it again.

Nagkaransa na sad ang byúda, The widow is back in action again.

Muiti (maiti) na sad ang mga sapà ning inita, The rivers will dry up again in this heat.

Muísa (maísa) na sad ang prisyu, The price is going up again.

Nagpabilib na sad ang hambugíru, The braggart is trying to impress us again.

Mamigwis na sad ang iring, The cat is going to have a litter again.

Nagpamàbà na sad ang maldíta níyang asáwa, His termagant wife is ranting at him again.

NA LANG NANG

Ipíis ko na lang nang ímung panúgun, I'll put your request in the postscript.

Kimua (ikimù) na lang nang ímung gikaun kay manlákat na ta, Eat your food down quickly because we're leaving.

Itsáhi nag tualya ang ímung buksidur kay gihímu na lang nang pantsing bag, Toss your boxer a towel.

Humaya (ihumay) na lang nang parsiláha, Just plant that parcel to rice.

Man

KA MAN LANG
Mangugat ka man lang dáyun, Just listen to reason.

Nagtayhad ka man lang dihà nga daghan mang buluhatun, You are just standing around when there many things to do.

Wà ka makakità sa pag-ági sa bátà kay nagtanghal ka man lang, You did not see the child pass by because you were just staring blankly.

Musiláub ka man lang dáyun, Say it calmly.

Nagrawraw ka man lang, Shut up!

Muputak ka man lang bísag wà kay lábut, Why do you butt in when I'm not talking to you?

Nalímut ka sa ímung túyù kay naghalhal ka man lang, You forgot what you went there for because you are scatterbrained.

Mualistu (maalistu) ka man lang ug makakità ug kwarta, You only move if you see money.

KA MAN SA
Mulatas ka man sa taliwálà sa mga táwung nagsultihánay, You have no manners.

Panghunaw kay milawgaw ka man sa pasaw, Wash your hands because you stirred the slop with them.

Istáring ka man sa wáli sa pári, You were conspicuously mentioned in the priest's sermon.

Makig-irgu ka man sa tindíra nga ímu man tung sayup, Why do you argue with the sales clerk when it was your fault?

Namali ka man sa ímung sinínà, You have your clothes on inside out.

KAY WA MAN

Nagtunguptúngup lang ko sa úras kay wà man kuy rilu, I'm just estimating the time because I don't have a watch.

Gitsíhan lang ko níya kay wà man kuy barku, She just snorted at me because I'm not rich (lit. have no ship).

Gisaylusaylúan lang ang akong mga papílis kay wà man ko muhátag ug bigay, My papers were just bypassed, because I didn't give any kickback.

Magpayà mi sa ámù kay wà man miy plátu, We use coconut shell plates because we don't have dishes.

Dì ka mutagad nákù kay wà man kuy náda nímu, You don't notice me because I am nothing to you.

Namatay ang tanum kay wà man gud bùbúi, The plant died because no one watered it.

Milimúk (nanlimúk) siya nákù kay wà man nákù pakapíha, She gave me a sour look because I did not allow her to copy mine.

Akuy milangkap sa íyang bayranan kay wà man siyay kwarta, I paid up all her obligations because she had no money.

Dúnay nagkubri sa akong amutan kay wà man ko paningli, S.o. paid for my obligation because nobody collected from me.

Maggútus na lang ta kay wà man giyuy sakyanan, We have to walk because there's no transportation.

DI KA MAN

Tunggul kaáyu nímu uy nga dì ka man makasabut ug sugúun, How stupid you are!

Dì ka man magtihiktíhik mangasábà, You scold without restraint.

Dì ka man giyung kahapit, You just keep going by our house, but you never drop in.

Pangsut kaáyu ka kay dì ka man manghúgas inig humag pangíhì, You smell because you don't wash yourself after.

Pa

SA DI PA
Mag-ílis úsà ko sa dì pa ta manglákaw, I'll change my clothes first before we go out.

Magsiyatsíyat únà ang mga magduduwà sa dì pa sugdan ang baskit, The players do practice shooting before the game starts.

Sa dinhà pa ko sa sirbisyu sa pulis, When I was working on the police force.

Mangluksu ang mga sundálu sa dì pa musanglad ang bards, The soldiers jump off before the barge hits the beach.

Manlukluk ta sa dì pa magpayring, Let's get out of the way before the firing starts.

WA PA KO
Wà pa ko níya hitsúi ug báyad, He has not paid me in full.

Walà untà ko muanhig wà pa ko imbitaha, I wouldn't have come unless I had been invited.

Wà pa ko makakatungà sa tísis, I have not reached the halfway point in my thesis.

Walà pa ko makasubmit sa ripurt, I have not yet handed in the report.

Human na ko makapaniudtu apan muribyu ko kay wà pa ko mabusug, I've already had my lunch, but I'll eat some more because I'm still hungry.

Wà pa ko makapamilyar nímu, I'm not familiar with you yet.

Walà pa ko makapalta sa akong klási, I never missed a class.

Wà pa ko mamalbas (manghimalbas), I haven't shaved yet.

Sukad ko makaalimatmat ug buut wà pa ko hibunali, I have not been spanked since the earliest time I can remember.

Wà pa ko kadumdum, I am a newcomer here.

UG WA PA

Nagprimíru na ang Marsu ug wà pa si Makuy, Here it is the first of March, and Macoy still hasn't come.

Sa panahun pa ni Mampur ang akong radiyu ug wà pa giyud magubà, My radio is as old as the hills and still in fine shape.

Maigù untà ko sa batu ug wà pa ko makaliput sa baril, I would have been hit with a stone if I had not ducked.

Makadahuldahul pa ning prutása ug wà pa pùpúa, This fruit would have grown bigger if it had not been picked so quickly.

Ug wà pa kay trátu, muaplay ko, If you have no boy friend, I'd like to apply.

WA PA GANI
Wà pa gániy úras, It hasn't even been an hour.

Nagbagìbì si Maríya kay walà pa gihápun ang íyang bána, Mary is ranting because her husband still isn't home.

Walà pa gánì mahinungà ang kan-un niíni, mitindug na kini, She got up before she finished her rice.

Wà pa gánì mubagting ag kampána mitayáda dáyun ang usang buksidur, Before the bell rang a boxer began striking.

Wà pa gánì siya makatarà, mibutu na ang pusil, The gun went off even before he could stop.

WA PA GIYUD

Ganíha ra nà siyang tábì wà pa giyud mutik-up ang bàbà, She has been chattering for quite some time now.

Wà pa giyud makatang-un ang kasábà sa gawas, The noise outside has not stopped.

Sa panahun pa ni Mampur ang akong radiyu ug wà pa giyud magubà, My radio is as old as the hills and still in fine shape.

Sígi lag bisíta, wà pa giyud makaispíking, He keeps visiting her but he hasn't proposed.

Nagkadisiutsu ka na lang wà pa giyud ka gihápuy buut, You are turning eighteen but still you are irresponsible.

Miáwas (naáwas) na lang síya sa kalindaryu, wà pa giyud maminyù, She is past thirty and still hasn't gotten married.

NGA WA PA

Ayaw kuhái ang sibúyas nga wà pa musipak (manipak), Don't harvest the leeks that haven't developed new bulbs.

Kaputlì nga walà pa kamansáhi sa kasinatían, Purity that has not been stained by experience.

Búhì kung pagtúu nga wà pa siya mamatay, I firmly believe he is still alive.

SA WA PA

Iyang hingpridiktahan ang súnug sa wà pa mahitabù, He predicted the fire before it happened.

Nakapaúlì siya sa wà pa mulibkas ang gúbat, He had a chance to go home before the war suddenly broke off.

Gidasunan ko níyag tubag sa wà pa ko makatiwas ug pangutána, He answered me immediately before I finished asking.

Nagkabayatbayat mig panghípus sa wà pa muabut ang mga bisíta, We were in a dither trying to clean up before the visit.

Exercise

Fill in the missing word with *na, man, or pa.*

Usdu ra kaáyu ang sulud sa kartun dì masira, The contents of the box are piled so high that the box can no longer held.

Usádu kaáyug dagway nang bayhána, That woman looks like she has already been used.

Usádu kaáyu ning ákù, I've got to buy a new pair of shoes.

Íya ning usarun (iusar) sininàa sa panarbáhu, He'll still wear this shirt to work.

Maáyu sag siya ray nagkarsúnis, It's good that he's wearing a shirt.

Udtu sad ming migíkan, It was already quite late when we left.

Gwápa sad, She is quite pretty.

Mahímù sad, It is quite possible.

Human sa unus, ang ulan say mibundak, After the squall, the rain came pouring down.

Nag-ulan sab, It's raining again.

Úsà kay akong tawgun, Just a second, because I'm going to call him.

Úsà gánì, Wait a minute, will you?

Ayaw úsag lakaw, Don't go for the while.

Mag-ílis úsà ko sa dì ta manglákaw, I'll change my clothes first before we go out.

Talagsa ka ra mamisíta nákù, You seldom visit me.

Magtagsatagsa lang tag pamaúlì, Let us now go home one by one.

Sanson panahun mauy usa ka táwu nga may ulusáhung kusug, Samson of ancient times was a of extraordinary strength.

Mag-uruyúruy ta kay wà tay ginikánan, Let us go easy on each other because we don't have parents anymore.

Mabúhì gihápun ta áning trabahúa, Oh, anyway, I can still make a living with this work.

Búhì uruy siya, He is still alive.

Naúrug run sa pagpalupad ug tabánug, Kiteflying is the latest fad.

Adtu mi, All right!

Nagkaurig nang bayhána human makasuway, That woman became lustful after she had experience.

Nagurganisar siya sa Lihiyun ni Maríya, She is organizing a Legion of Mary unit.

Sa nadúgay , naurdinaryu lang ang taas nga buhuk, After some time it became an ordinary thing to have.

Haduul ang úras sa masakitun, The sick man's hour is close at hand.

Lingsud nga nag-uráray sa tiilans búkid, A town nestled at the foot of a mountain.

Urálun ta lang ning sinugbang isdà kay walà may kan-un, Let's just eat the broiled fish alone because there's no more rice.

Nagkaupus ang íyang kinabúhì, His life is slowly coming to an end.

Naupus ang akong paílub, My patience has come to an end.

Wà giyuy lingawlíngaw, All I do is work.

Maupisyal gánì ang ímung apuwintmint, Once your appointment becomes official.

Nagkaupay ang akong mga núka, My scabies are healing.

Up ko, I'm off duty now.

Unyúnan lang nátù ang íyang sugyut, Let's agree to his suggestion.

Dì ko mag-unung sa kasábà ni Nánay kay ági lang nà, I don't mind Mother's scolding because it won't last.

May hatagunun diay ko nímu, Oh, I still have s.t. to give you.

Giunuran sad ang íyang láwas, He has gotten flesh back on his body.

Ákù ta kang giunúhan, ha, Watch out.

Ug mauntup ra ning akong kwarta pára pamilíti wà kuy ikapaínit, If my money is just enough for my fare, then I won't have any way to get there.

Muuntul-untul mulakaw ang tagabúkid bísan ug pátag , Mountaineers bounce as they walk, even in the lowland.

Miuntul ang akong gitun-an, dì masulud sa akong úlu, The things I studied won't register in my head.

Lima ka búlan ning batáa apan giuntuhan , The baby is only five months old but she already has upper teeth.

Ug ugmà giyud ang kasal naghíkay tà run, If the wedding were really going to be tomorrow.

Dílì aku, kayg aku , nahuman tà run, It wasn’t me, because if it were, it would have been done now.

Ug aku , mahuman tà run, I could have gotten it done, if I were to have been the one to do it.

Walà untà ko muanhig wà ko imbitaha, I wouldn’t have come unless I had been invited.

Nindut tà ug nadala nímu, It would have been nice if you had brought it.

Mugíkan untà siya apan mibagyu, He was about to leave but there was a storm.

Unsáun ug dì magpatúu, dì hilatiguhan, I couldn’t help it.

Mga bínu, tubà, sirbísa, ug unsa kadtu (dihà), Wine, toddy, beer, and what have you.

Unsa, human ba, wà , Say, is it done or not?

Unmumintu, maglipstik lang ko, Just a second, I'll put lipstick on.

Wà ka makaunminútu ug sulti, You haven't talked for a minute.

Unguyan kaáyu sa trabáhu nang tawhána kay tapulan gud, That man can't endure work because he is lazy.

Nag-ungut ang kwáku sa bàbà sa tigúwang, There was a pipe stuck in the old man's mouth.

Naghilak ka tingáli, kay nag-ungus-ungus ka , úngut - unsa You must have been crying because you are sniffling.

Mag-ungaw gánì ang akong kwarta sa kahurutun, mukáun lang ko ug buwad, When my money is nearly gone I resort to eating dried fish.

Giundángan siya sa íyang dugù, Her menstruation has stopped.

Hiundanan (naundanan) níya ang íyang sayup, He has just realized his mistakes.

Kanúnay siyang makakitag áway kay unaunahun , He always finds himself in a fight because he is a trouble-maker.

Dúna kuy hatagun nímu, I still have s.t. to give you.

Kun dílì mahímung sultíhun ang átung gikasungían, átù lang awáyun, If we can't settle our differences by talking, we'll fight.

Lulúhun ko ang tigúwang, I will call the old man Grandfather.

Ugmáun lang nà nákù, I will just do that tomorrow.

Giumuyan ang akong buktun, My arm has gathered strength again.

Dì giyud ko makaumuy paglakaw, I have no more strength to go out.

Paumúka lang siyag katulog kay Duminggu run, Allow her to sleep in because it's Sunday.

Pumipirma untà siya sa kuntrátu, He was just about to sign the contract.

Umuulì ko, I am about to go home.

Didtu sa uspital maumpawi ang nakuyapan, The who fainted came to in the hospital.

Sa kaapíki sa mga buluhatun sa panimalay naumnis lang ang akong paniudtu, I was so busy with the housework that I missed my meal.

Umil kaáyu ning pinipíga, The rice crunch has gotten all soggy.

Ang libintadur nga muumidu (maumidu) dì mubutu, A firecracker that gets moist won't explode.

Aku ang nag-ulus sa ímung lápis, I borrowed your pencil.

Dad-un si Pína sa matirniti kay giul-ulan , Bring Pina to the hospital because she has labor pains.

Iúlug nang bukag kay adtu ta, Please put the basket on my head because we're going now.

Sag-ulúhun ko lang ang paniudtu, I'll just skip lunch.

Daginutan kaáyu ning bayhána kay ang ultimung mumhu hipúsun , This woman is very thrifty.

Ultima lang ning akong pag-anhi dinhi, This will be my last visit here.

Ayawg binátà kay ulitáwu ka , Don't be childish.

Ulitáwung gúlang, An old bachelor.

Maúlit siya ug kataw-an, She'll become angry if they laugh at her.

Nagkaulipun ka sa ímung bisyu, You are becoming a slave to your vices.

Ulimpiyánun (iulimpiyan) ko untà ang akong kasal, nabakyà hinúun, I want to keep my wedding quiet and simple, but the news has spread.

Nangulílang ka sa paniudtu, You are late for dinner.

Lisud atimanun ning tigúlang nga maghingulì (gihingulian), It's difficult to look after an old man who is in his second childhood.

Nag-úlì mi human sa ámung panagbángì, We are on good terms again after our quarrel.

Dì sà mi muúlì sa ámung lisinsiya kay wà miy babáyi, We won't stop having babies until we have a girl.

Ngánung gipakauláwan mu aku, Why did you put me to shame?

Miúlat (naulat) ang akong samad, My wound has formed a scar.

Kalígù lang kun hiulanan (maulanan) ka, Take a bath if you get caught in the rain.

Ulahia (iulahi) lang ang uban nga dì madala, Just leave those things you cannot take along behind.

Ulahi ka kaáyu sa paniudtu, You are very late for dinner.

Giulágan ang bigal sa butakal, The boar served the sow.

Ukupádu kaáyu ang átung sakyanan, Our bus is already full.

Ayaw ukun-ukúna (iukun-úkun) ang ímung pagdáwat, ábi lang wà ka kaayun, Don't hesitate to accept it or else they will think you're not ready.

Karun nga pakantáhun untà, midumílì hinúun, Now that it was time to sing, he refused.

Gustu lang kung muuk-uk sa kaúlaw, I wanted to shrink into the floorboards with shame.

Miúkub ang kula, The glue has set.

Wà nay lugar nga uktabáhun (iuktába) ang inyung kasal, There's no more time for your wedding to be postponed.

Muukpaw ang linakwan sa táwung naánad ug puyù sa búkid bísan ug mapátag ang laktan, People who are used to the mountains bounce when they walk, even on leveled surface.

Nagpaábut sa íyang úki, Still waiting for his approval.

Dílì siya makaukang sa kwadru nga gilansang sa bongbong, He can no longer bite the cage that is nailed to the wall.

Dì siya maukal sa pagkamaistru, He can't be removed from his teaching post.

Ukala nang bátà sa íyang inahan, Take that child away from its mother.

Nagkaukal ang pintal sa dáang balay, The paint of the old house is peeling off.

Wà muukal (maukal) ang unud sa lubi, The coconut meat has not detached from its shell.

Úhù kay nagkaun ko, Just a minute.

Ug uhù da , miguwang mananáug si Ilurdi, As expected, Elorde came out the winner.

Uhú, dáan lagi ko, Aha!

Uhú, sayup pud ka, Aha, you made a mistake again.

Miuhay (nanguhay, giuhayan) ang átung humay, Our rice is bearing panicles now.

Was that difficult? Compare.

Usdu ra kaáyu ang sulud sa kartun dì na masira, The contents of the box are piled so high that the box can no longer held.

Usádu na kaáyug dagway nang bayhána, That woman looks like she has already been used.

Usádu na kaáyu ning ákù, I've got to buy a new pair of shoes.

Íya pa ning usarun (iusar) sininâa sa panarbáhu, He'll still wear this shirt to work.

Maáyu man sag siya ray nagkarsúnis, It's good that he's wearing only a shirt.

Udtu na sad ming migíkan, It was already quite late when we left.

Gwápa man sad, She is quite pretty.

Mahímù man sad, It is quite possible.

Human sa unus, ang ulan na say mibundak, After the squall, the rain came pouring down.

Nag-ulan na sab, It's raining again.

Ug ikíha ko níya, ikíha ko sab siya, If he sues me, I'll sue him in turn.

Úsà pa kay akong tawgun, Just a second, because I'm going to call him.

Úsà pa gánì, Wait a minute, will you?

Ayaw úsag lakaw, Don't go for the while.

Mag-ílis úsà ko sa dì pa ta manglákaw, I'll change my clothes first before we go out.

Talagsa ka ra man mamisíta nákù, You seldom visit me.

Magtagsatagsa na lang tag pamaúlì, Let us now go home one by one.

Sanson panahun mauy usa ka táwu nga may ulusáhung kusug, Samson of ancient times was a man of extraordinary strength.

Usa sad siya sa mungadtu, He is also a member of the group going there.

Mag-uruyúruy ta kay wà na tay ginikánan, Let us go easy on each other because we don't have parents anymore.

Mabúhì man gihápun ta áning trabahúa, Oh, anyway, I can still make a living with this work.

Búhì pa uruy siya, He is still alive.

Naúrug na run sa pagpalupad ug tabánug, Kiteflying is the latest fad.

Adtu na mi, All right!

Nagkaurig na nang bayhána human makasuway, That woman became lustful after she had experience.

Nagurganisar pa siya sa Lihiyun ni Maríya, She is organizing a Legion of Mary unit.

Sa nadúgay na, naurdinaryu na lang ang taas nga buhuk, After some time it became an ordinary thing to have.

Haduul na ang úras sa masakitun, The sick man's hour is close at hand.

Lingsud nga nag-uráray sa tiilans búkid, A town nestled at the foot of a mountain.

Urálun ta na lang ning sinugbang isdà kay walà na may kan-un, Let's just eat the broiled fish alone because there's no more rice.

Nagkaupus na ang íyang kinabúhì, His life is slowly coming to an end.

Naupus na ang akong paílub, My patience has come to an end.

Wà na giyuy lingawlíngaw, All I do is work.

Maupisyal na gánì ang ímung apuwintmint, Once your appointment becomes official.

Nagkaupay na ang akong mga núka, My scabies are healing.

Up na ko, I'm off duty now.

Unyúnan na lang nátù ang íyang sugyut, Let's agree to his suggestion.

Dì ko mag-unung sa kasábà ni Nánay kay ági man lang nà, I don't mind Mother's scolding because it won't last.

May hatagunun pa diay ko nímu, Oh, I still have s.t. to give you.

Nangúrug ang akong kaunuran sa kalágut, My flesh trembled in anger.

Giunuran na sad ang íyang láwas, He has gotten flesh back on his body.

Ákù ta na kang giunúhan, ha, Watch out.

Ug mauntup ra ning akong kwarta pára pamilíti wà na kuy ikapaínit, If my money is just enough for my fare, then I won't have any way to get there.

Muuntul-untul mulakaw ang tagabúkid bísan ug pátag na, Mountaineers bounce as they walk, even in the lowland.

Miuntul ang akong gitun-an, dì na masulud sa akong úlu, The things I studied won't register in my head.

Lima pa ka búlan ning batáa apan giuntuhan na, The baby is only five months old but she already has upper teeth.

Ug ugmà pa giyud ang kasal naghíkay tà run, If the wedding were really going to be tomorrow.

Dílì aku, kayg aku pa, nahuman na tà run, It wasn't me, because if it were, it would have been done now.

Ug aku pa, mahuman na tà run, I could have gotten it done, if I were to have been the one to do it.

Walà untà ko muanhig wà pa ko imbitaha, I wouldn't have come unless I had been invited.

Nindut tà ug nadala pa nímu, It would have been nice if you had brought it.

Mugíkan na untà siya apan mibagyu, He was about to leave but there was a storm.

Unsáun man ug dì magpatúu, dì hilatiguhan, I couldn't help it.

Mga bínu, tubà, sirbísa, ug unsa pa kadtu (dihà), Wine, toddy, beer, and what have you.

Unsa, human na ba, wà pa, Say, is it done or not?

Unmumintu, maglipstik na lang ko, Just a second, I'll put lipstick on.

Wà pa ka makaunminútu ug sulti, You haven't talked for a minute.

Unguyan kaáyu sa trabáhu nang tawhána kay tapulan man gud, That man can't endure work because he is lazy.

Nag-ungut ang kwáku sa bàbà sa tigúwang, There was a pipe stuck in the old man's mouth.

Naghilak ka man tingáli, kay nag-ungus-ungus ka man, úngut – unsa You must have been crying because you are sniffling.

Mag-ungaw na gánì ang akong kwarta sa kahurutun, mukáun na lang ko ug buwad, When my money is nearly gone I resort to eating dried fish.

Giundángan na siya sa íyang dugù, Her menstruation has stopped.

Hiundanan (naundanan) na níya ang íyang sayup, He has just realized his mistakes.

Kanúnay siyang makakitag áway kay unaunahun man, He always finds himself in a fight because he is a trouble-maker.

Dúna pa kuy hatagun nímu, I still have s.t. to give you.

Kun dílì mahímung sultíhun ang átung gikasungían, átù na lang awáyun, If we can't settle our differences by talking, we'll fight.

Lulúhun ko ang tigúwang, I will call the old man Grandfather.

Ugmáun na lang nà nákù, I will just do that tomorrow.

Giumuyan na ang akong buktun, My arm has gathered strength again.

Dì na giyud ko makaumuy paglakaw, I have no more strength to go out.

Paumúka lang siyag katulog kay Duminggu man run, Allow her to sleep in because it's Sunday.

Pumipirma na untà siya sa kuntrátu, He was just about to sign the contract.

Umuulì na ko, I am about to go home.

Didtu na sa uspital maumpawi ang nakuyapan, The man who fainted came to in the hospital.

Sa kaapíki sa mga buluhatun sa panimalay naumnis na lang ang akong paniudtu, I was so busy with the housework that I missed my meal.

Umil na kaáyu ning pinipíga, The rice crunch has gotten all soggy.

Ang libintadur nga muumidu (maumidu) dì na mubutu, A firecracker that gets moist won't explode.

Aku ang nag-ulus sa ímung lápis, I borrowed your pencil.

Dad-un na si Pína sa matirniti kay giul-ulan na, Bring Pina to the hospital because she has labor pains.

Iúlug na nang bukag kay adtu na ta, Please put the basket on my head because we're going now.

Sag-ulúhun ko na lang ang paniudtu, I'll just skip lunch.

Daginutan kaáyu ning bayhána kay ang ultimung mumhu hipúsun pa, This woman is very thrifty.

Ultima na lang ning akong pag-anhi dinhi, This will be my last visit here.

Ayawg binátà kay ulitáwu ka na, Don't be childish.

Ulitáwung gúlang, An old bachelor.

Maúlit na siya ug kataw-an, She'll become angry if they laugh at her.

Nagkaulipun ka sa ímung bisyu, You are becoming a slave to your vices.

Ulimpiyánun (iulimpiyan) ko untà ang akong kasal, nabakyà man hinúun, I want to keep my wedding quiet and simple, but the news has spread.

Nangulílang ka na sa paniudtu, You are late for dinner.

Lisud atimanun ning tigúlang nga maghingulì (gihingulian) na, It's difficult to look after an old man who is in his second childhood.

Nag-úlì na mi human sa ámung panagbángì, We are on good terms again after our quarrel.

Dì sà mi muúlì sa ámung lisinsiya kay wà pa miy babáyi, We won't stop having babies until we have a girl.

Ngánung gipakauláwan mu man aku, Why did you put me to shame?

Miúlat (naulat) na ang akong samad, My wound has formed a scar.

Kalígù na lang kun hiulanan (maulanan) ka, Take a bath if you get caught in the rain.

Ulahia (iulahi) na lang ang uban nga dì na madala, Just leave those things you cannot take along behind.

Ulahi ka na kaáyu sa paniudtu, You are very late for dinner.

Giulágan na ang bigal sa butakal, The boar served the sow.

Ukupádu na kaáyu ang átung sakyanan, Our bus is already full.

Ayaw ukun-ukúna (iukun-úkun) ang ímung pagdáwat, ábi pa lang wà ka kaayun, Don't hesitate to accept it or else they will think you're not ready.

Karun nga pakantáhun na untà, midumílì na hinúun, Now that it was time to sing, he refused.

Gustu na lang kung muuk-uk sa kaúlaw, I wanted to shrink into the floorboards with shame.

Miúkub na ang kula, The glue has set.

Wà nay lugar nga uktabáhun (iuktába) pa ang inyung kasal, There's no more time for your wedding to be postponed.

Muukpaw ang linakwan sa táwung naánad ug puyù sa búkid bísan ug mapátag na ang laktan, People who are used to the mountains bounce when they walk, even on leveled surface.

Nagpaábut pa sa íyang úki, Still waiting for his approval.

Dílì na siya makaukang sa kwadru nga gilansang sa bongbong, He can no longer bite the cage that is nailed to the wall.

Dì na siya maukal sa pagkamaistru, He can't be removed from his teaching post.

Ukala na nang bátà sa íyang inahan, Take that child away from its mother.

Nagkaukal na ang pintal sa dáang balay, The paint of the old house is peeling off.

Wà pa muukal (maukal) ang unud sa lubi, The coconut meat has not detached from its shell.

Úhù pa kay nagkaun pa ko, Just a minute.

Ug uhù da man, miguwang mananáug si Ilurdi, As expected, Elorde came out the winner.

Uhú, dáan pa lagi ko, Aha!

Uhú, sayup na pud ka, Aha, you made a mistake again.

Miuhay (nanguhay, giuhayan) na ang átung humay, Our rice is bearing panicles now.

Challenge

In the following rough of the short story, *Ang Ducati nga Babaye,* that I have written a while back, you will fill in any word you have practiced so far which seems the best fit. Please note that all u(s) have been upgraded to o(s), for the modern spelling. The old spelling is still widely used in social media posts, but are less frequent on news outlets. The Cebuano language is no longer taught even in public schools, therefore people simply take a phonetic approach where few rules are evident.

Ang Ducati nga Babaye

ISBN: 9781981021130
Villaggio Publishing Ltd

Bahin 1

GABUN, SMOG, SINGGIT mga tawo; ang bugtong butang nga naa akong hunahuna mao ang kalibog. Pagkalibog alang mga butang nga walay kahulogan. Gihunahuna Dios ang mga tawo, gisultihan sila paglakaw ngadto disyerto. Didto siya, nagtindog didto. Ang kabukiran disyerto nagsunod pagkalapad niining komplikado nga yuta nga gipamulak pagkawalay kaluoy bulkan, akong mga kalihokan, nga hapit mapalayo alang maayo--unta.

Nagdrayb ko, oo, layo tanang butang nga akong gitukod, ang tanan nga akong naangkon, mga butang nga walay kahulong.

Ang mga zebra (marka trapiko) hapsay nga gipintalan, mga nanambong nga mitabok, mga simbolo trapiko nga nagpagrabe kinabuhi; pagluwas katawhan uban mga semiotics? Tingali usa kini ka pagbati. Ang kakulangan kagawasan.

Ang mga estudyante milaktaw klase, ang bintana sakyanan gipaubos, sama kanunay, ang hangin mahinungdanon; Huwebes , sila nagsaulog. Pagsaulog nila unsa? Unsa gayud ang kalainan tali mga singgit mga tawo mga singgit mga mananap?

Tingali dili sila mga estudyante, gibalibaran nila ang mga hairdos nagsul-ob sila mga kupo. Ang usa nagalabay iyang kupo hangin, siya adunay epileptic nga dagway, siya nagdagan aron pagsugat usa ka babaye, lain nga itom puti nga talan-awon, laing konsepto gugma nga dili matukib, oo sila pagkatinuod mga apan kini nagsamok kanako usa ka gamay; Siguradong pamilyar siya nako-dili siya. Kinsa siya? Kini usa ka ting-ulan nga adlaw, o dili; tingali nag-ulan lang usa ka oras wala , tingali kini ulan usa ka gatus ka tuig ang milabay.

Ako panihapon uban akong pamilya, katapusan. Ang sulugoon naghatag kanako sulat; Usa lang kini ka pahina, tulo ka mga pulong: Moabot ako ugma. Kon wala nimo makilala si Jenny kaniadto, pasidan?siya makalignaw kaayo. Siya adunay tulo ka mga pagbati: Ducatis, hilig, psychoanalysis. Ang katapusan nga usa mao ang usa ka gamay annoyance kadaghanan mga kalag nga magpalayo gikan iyang tungod niana nga hinungdan. Kini usa ka misteryo alang kanako kung giunsa siya adunay usa labing makapaikag nga pagkinabuhi alang usa ka babaye iyang edad. Uban usa ka makalingaw nga tête-à-tête, daghan nga marmol, siya nakahimo pagtukod usa ka talagsaon nga Tuscan-style nga villa uban sulud gawas mga olympic swimming pool usa labing inila nga kasilinganan La Jolla, California.

Makaiikag, siya dili gayud balay. Nagdrayb siya iyang Ducati nga adunay tambok nga pitaka likod iyang pantalon. akong kahibalo, wala siyay bisan unsang pitaka iyang gitamay ang mga aksesorya batang babaye. Uban iyang foppish nga reputasyon iyang nakabungkag daghang mga kasingkasing, pipila ka mga bukog usab; siya walay hingpit nga interes alang usa ka makanunayon nga relasyon, ngadto kaniya, ang gugma nga mga kauban mao lamang ang makalingaw.

Busa, unsa karon? Ang sulud nga babaye nagtutok kang Jenny nga anaa tanaman nagbasa usa ka makalilisang nga basahon; Wala ako makakita iyang pagbasa kaniadto, gawas nga dili ko maghunahuna nga ang ingon nga genre nahisubay iyang dautan nga intelihensya. Ngano nga siya motutok kaniya sama niana, aduna bay butang alang usag usa, usa ka butang nga wala nako mahibaloi? Nagatindog siya mga kahoy, unsay iyang gibuhat? Nagtan-aw mga pantalon ni Jenny?

Tingali ang pagtan-aw ni Mela libro nga Jenny naghupot wala gani magbasa. Dili, dili OK nga usbon ang hilisgutan.

Hikalimti kini, naningkamot siya nga makuha ang iyang pagtagad; dili, si Jenny naningkamot pagkuha iyang pagtagad, oh dili, wala gyud siya nagsalikway kaniya karon. Maayo siya. Siya natugaw, karon siya mikalagiw nga wala diha sulod balay, dili siya maayo nga magdadagan, dili siya maayo daghang mga butang. Anaa siya atubangan usa ka salamin, pagtuon mga postura, pagdayeg iyang kaugalingon; Gikuha niya ang usa ka ariyos, karon iyang giwagtang ang laing usa. Siya dili matagbaw; siya ang nagbutang kanila balik. Ang iyang mga ngabil, oo iyang gihikap ang iyang mga ngabil; sila mga manipis, lawasnon. Wala siya pahiyom. Dan, siya balik tanaman, naglakaw siya sagbut sama usa ka baliw, siya naghuyop usa ka sungkod; usa ka bag-ong double bubble nga teorya? Wala siya mahibalo kung unsa ang impyerno nga iyang gihunahuna. Siya adunay tan-aw iyang nawong, naghilak siya, nagtan-aw usab siya kang Jenny, kinsa nahibal-an, tingali siya nahimo uban kaniya. Nagdagan siya sulod balay uban kabuang, siya anaa kusina, ang gas hose, iyang gibira ang gas hose gikan stove gibutang kini iyang baba. Naghimo siya og pipila ka aerosol, apan adunay problema nga pagginhawa. Siya buang, oh Dios, siya gayud buang, nahimo niya kini kaniadto. Ako adunay pagbati nga gusto niya nga patyon ang iyang kaugalingon. OK, naa siya salog, apan si Jenny matud , akong hunahuna siya nagtan-aw niini nga sine kaniadto; Nagdalagan siya sulod, gipili siya niya sama usa ka rag nga monyeka; Giguyod niya siya ngadto kwarto.

"Hoy, ikaw ba ang tanan?" Nangutana siya.

Siya naglingolingo iyang ulo pipila ka mga higayon; nahibal-an niya kung unsaon kini buhaton. Talagsaon siya. Siya nagatutok kaniya; siya natunaw.

Dili siya makasulti og usa ka pulong, nagbag-o siya iyang hunahuna.

"Oo, tanan, tanan." Si Mela mitubag.

"Tinuod?" Si Jenny nangutana.

"Oo." Si Mela mitubag.

"Gihatagan mo ako kalisang," si Jenny miingon.

"Dili, wala ako." Si Mela mitubag.

"Nganong gibuhat nimo kana?" Si Jenny nangutana.

"Tungod usa ka tawo ang gusto akong utok." Si Mela mitubag.

"Kinsa?" Si Jenny nangutana.

"Usa ka higala." Si Mela mitubag.

"Komosta ako?" Si Jenny nangutana.

"Ikaw usab." Si Mela mitubag.

"Ikaw buang!" Si Jenny miingon.

"Numero uno ba ako? Si Mela nangutana.

Iyang gipahigda siya iyang higdaanan, usa ka babaye. Si Mela nagbira sinina, unsay iyang gibuhat? Gidapit ba siya niya?

Dili, dili siya interesado. Dili siya malipayon, wala siya makasabut usa ka butang. Siya nag-ayo iyang sinina, gipatapik niya ang iyang buhok, naghilak siya, gihagkan niya ang iyang kamot; Oh Dios ko, siya gayud ang misulod niini. Ang mga mata ni Jenny dako, gamhanan. Gipaduol niya kini. OK, naa siya ibabaw niya, naluoy ba siya alang niya? Nag-agi sila usa ka gamay, siya nagpadayon pagpugong batok iyang crotch, nahibal-an niya kung unsaon kini buhaton.

Karon siya malipayon.

?

Nagahigda ako. Dili ako, dili, ako nagsul-ob og pajama; dili kini iya. Aw, mangatulog usab kita. Dili ko. Buweno, niining higayona ako mahimo usab nga maglakaw gawas makaginhawa presko nga hangin, sans veils; oh oo, kaadlawon kaayo, apan kung wala nimo nakit-an, nagtuo ako nga nagkagrabe. Ngano? Wala ako masayud. Kini mahitabo kanatong tanan usahay kinabuhi. Makahahadlok kini; Namatikdan nako nga duha ka mga babaye ang natulog usa ka higdaanan lawak sala. Jenny, ang Ducati nga babaye; Dili ako sigurado kung kinsa ang usa; Sandra, akong primogeniture. Dili ko tugutan ang mga kalihokan homosexual sulod akong balay, dili kini ang pulo Sappho; Manghinaut ako nga wala ako'y hunahuna dili makakita, tingali natulog ko. Buweno, mangatulog kita balik, si Anna wala makamatikod usa ka butang, maayo alang kaniya; dili siya kinahanglan nga makakita kanako ingon nga kahimtang.

Kini opisyal, ako nasakit, ako usa ka tawong masakiton. si Sandra, ang akong anak nga babaye sunod kanako samtang ako naghigda. Ang akong lawas dili masakiton, apan ang akong hunahuna mao. Dili kini makita ni Sandra; Si Jenny naglakaw lang siya nagtutok kanako, ang iyang pahiyom nagsulti kanako usa ka butang. Tingali ako kinahanglan nga mangutana kaniya. Alang mga rekord, si Jenny usa ko ka estudyante, usa ka talagsaon nga usa ka tawo dihang ako usa ka puli nga magtutudlo. Gikuha niya ang habol gihatagan niya ako og usa ka tiil pagmasahe; Si Sandra wala gisulti usa ka pulong, apan iyang gisundan ang mga lihok ni Jenny uban iyang maalamon nga mga mata; Kinahanglan nga sila magkahiusa; ang akong anak nga lalaki nga si Mark nakapaamgo kanako niana. Gipataas ni Jenny ang akong mga bitiis; Nakita nako nga kini usa ka matang rejuvenating therapy nga iyang nakat-unan Europe uban iyang gang motorsiklo. Aw, usa ka paagi, maayo ang akong gibati.

Oo, usa ka semana karon, ako nagsugod pagbati nga mas maayo, hapit laing lalaki. Ang tawo nga gusto nakong mahimo; Dili, tingali dili , wala . Adunay usa ka kaaway sulod nako, kinsa ?

Oh oo, usa ka biyahe ngadto nasud; Nagdrayb si Jenny sama usa ka baliw, nahigugma siya iyang Ducati; apan niining higayona ako kinahanglan gayud nga mosulti kaniya unsa ang nahitabo, kini usa ka moral nga butang. Oo, gisultihan ko siya nga adunay kalibog akong hunahuna takna kinahanglan ko nga makuha kini gikan akong dughan. Wala ko makasulti og usa ka pulong, apan siya malipayon, kana nakapalipay kanako; pamahaw pagsakay lanaw, ingon og usa ka maayong ideya.

"Suginli ako Jenny, unsay among gikaon?" Nangutana ko.

"Dili ako ang gigutom, apan ako magabantay kanimo; kanunay ka nga makalingaw uban kutsilyo kakha imong mga kamot; Makakuha ako'g inspirasyon pagpamalandong imong mga pagduhaduha." Si Jenny mitubag.

"Naa ba ako kasamok?" Nangutana ko.

"Wala ako masayud. Anaa ka ba kasamok?" Si Jenny mitubag.

"Nawad-an ka dula." Miingon ko.

"Ganahan ko imong mga pulong." Si Jenny miingon.

"Ganahan ko imong buhok." Miingon ko.

Sige, pamahaw , karon gyud ang panahon pagsulti kaniya unsa ang problema. Siya nagdagan, siya kusog; siya tulin nga paspas, diin ang impyerno nagdagan siya? OK, nakit-an ko siya; siya nahugno yuta siya nagtutok kalangitan; Kanunay niya kanang buhaton tanaman campus.

Mm, kinahanglan nga mao ra nga libro. Suginli ako Jenny, unsay imong gibasa?

"Gihaylo mo ako, imo akong gipanag-iya, miabot ka, ikaw nakadaug. Karon kinahanglan kong tawagon ang akong kaugalingon nga usa ka butang nga pagyubit. Ang akong suod nga mga higala nakasaksi akong pagkapukan." Siya nagbasa.

"Kinsa ang nagsulat niana?" Nangutana ko.

"Ang mga pulong mas importante magsusulat. Kinahanglan nga hubaron magbabasa ang mga pulong nga gusto niya. Kini usa ka moral nga butang." Si Jenny miingon.

"Sa akong hunahuna wala ang ingon nga mga pulong gisulat alang usa ka partikular nga rason gawas—" Gipasabut ko.

"Gawas?" Si Jenny mitubag.

"Kalimti kini." Miingon ko.

"Husto ka; Wala nako mabasa ang mga pulong aron pagsulti kanimo kamatuoran." Si Jenny miignon.

"Mangadto ta balay." Miingon ko.

?

Ang postman nahibalik, nakahatag siya og laing sulat ngadto kang Mela, ang sulugoon. Gihatag lang niya kini kanako; Kinahanglan nga kini usa ka bon vivant ugma, kinsay mahimo? Walay usa nga moabot; wala kini gitumong kanako."

"Jenny, kini alang nimo." Miingon ko.

Gitan-aw ni Jenny ang sulat.

"OK, kinahanglan kong mobiya ugma." Siya miingon.

Bahin 2

Panahon:17:00

"Jenny, dili ka kinahanglan nga mobiya." Si Anna miingon.

"Nahadlok ko nga kinahanglan ko." Si Jenny mitubag.

"Dili, dili ko nimo tugutan." Miinsistir si Anna.

"Usa ka adlaw o duha, unsa ang kalainan?" Si Jenny nangutana.

"Sukad nga ikaw miabot niini nga balay ang tanan nausab, ako nausab, imong giablihan?" Gipatin-aw ni Anna.

"Anna, hunong, palihug." Si Jenny miingon.

"Dili, mao kini kung unsa kini; Nakaamgo ko karon nga ang akong bana dili gayud ang tawo nga akong gihigugma ?" Si Anna miingon.

"Dili, wala ako moanhi tungod niana nga hinungdan." Gibalda ni Jenny.

"Kinahanglan nga paminawon mo ako." Si Anna miingon.

"Unsa ang iyang mga sayup?" Si Jenny nangutana.

"Sa akong hunahuna ang iyang mga sayop mao ang akong sayop." Si Anna mitubag.

"Niini nga kahimtang wala ka'y problema." Gipatin-aw ni Jenny.

"Ako buang." Si Anna miingon.

"Dili, kinahanglan nga dili ka." Si Jenny miingon.

"Gidumtan nako ang akong kaugalingon ang tanan nga naglibut kanako." Si Anna miingon.

"Dili, dili kinahanglan." Si Jenny miingon.

"Naghunahuna ba kamo nga ako iya kalibutan?" Si Anna nangutana.

"Maayo kini nga pangutana." Si Jenny mitubag.

"Naghunahuna ka ba nga makapabilin ka og gamay?" Si Anna nangutana.

"Ngano?" Si Jenny nangutana.

"Dili ko gustong mamatay nga wala nimo." Si Anna mitubag.

"Ikaw mabuhi hangtud kahangturan." Si Jenny miingon.

"Sa unsang paagi ka makasiguro?" Si Anna nangutana.

Aduna ka'y aura kaalam, usa ka aura tinguha, gipanalanginan ka taas nga kinabuhi." Si Jenny mitubag.

"Nagahatag ka ba kanako og usa ka pagbasa? Ikaw usa ka babaye nga daghang mga talento, apan ako nagduhaduha mahitungod niining butang nga aura, dili ko kini makita." Si Anna miingon.

"Ang imong aura usa ka butang nga dili nimo makita, apan ang uban imong palibot." Gipatin-aw ni Jenny.

Panahon 18:00

"Utang ko kanimo ang kalibutan. Ang tanan nga imo ginhatag akon. Karon nagtuo ko nga ang kinabuhi adunay kahulugan. Naghunahuna ako nga gidumtan nako ang mga babaye, tungod gidumtan nako ang akong inahan. Karon ang tanan lahi, Jenny, ang tanan klaro kaayo. Ang tanan?" Si Mark miingon.

"Ang tanan maayo, Mark; ang tanan maayo. Ang imong inahan nahigugma kanimo. Sila nahigugma kanimo dinhi niining balaya." Si Jenny miingon.

"Ug gihigugma ko ikaw. Akong buhaton." Si Mark miingon.

"Ug ako nahigugma usab kanimo, apan kinahanglan nimo nga masabtan." Si Jenny miingon.

"Dili, dili ko tugutan nga makasabut, ang akong kasingkasing dili motugot kanako." Si Mark miingon.

"Adunay usa ka bag-ong sakit tibuok kalibutan." Gipatin-aw ni Jenny.

"Pakigsulti kanako, unsa kini?" Si Mark nangutana.

"Nahadlok ka ba gugma?" Si Jenny nangutana.

"Nahadlok ko nga magul-anon kaayo." Si Mark mitubag.

"Niini nga kaso ang usa ka estatuwa mao ang tubag?" Si Jenny miingon.

"Ang imong estatuwa, ang Ducati girl nga estatuwa, akong simbahon kini ingon nga diyosa, diha mismo akong kwarto, apan nahadlok ko nga ang usa ka estatuwa mahimong magpasabut katapusan kinabuhi." Si Mark mitubag.

"Ingna ko; unsa ang akong sayop, nga ania dinhi?" Si Mark nangutana.

Panahon 19:00

"Wala ko mahibal-an ang gugma wala nako gigahin kining talagsaon nga mga hapon kauban nimo. Ang tanan nahigugma kanimo, ang akong mga higala dili makahunong nga makig-istorya kanimo dili ako makatulog nga dili maghunahuna kanimo. Unsay imong gibuhat nako?" Si Sandra nangutana.

"Unsa ang akong nahimo kanimo, Sandra?" Si Jenny nangutana.

"Ikaw ang una nga naghisgot mahitungod gugma. usa ka paagi, gipahayag mo ang giyera akong kalag." Si Sanda mitubag.

"Uh, nga kinahanglan nga makahadlok." Si Jenny miingon.

"Sa sinugdan, apan karon nga nakaila ko nimo, dili ko mahadlok." Si Sandra miingon.

"Ang akong tingali mao ang pagpakita kanimo

dalan." Si Jenny miingon.

"Ug ang kapalaran, unsa ang akong padulngan kon wala ka? Unsa ang gugma, laing matang kanser nga walay tambal? Ingna ko." Si Sandra nangutana.

"Kinahanglan kong moadto." Si Jenny miingon.

"Dili, ayaw ko biya-i!" Misinggit si Sandra.

"Ihatag ko kanimo ang usa ka kopa nga kape." Si Jenny miingon.

"Dili, palihug paminawa ako." Si Sandra miingon.

"Kinahanglan nga magsul-ob ka dili magbagtok ang imong inahan pultahan." Gitambagan ni Jenny.

"Si Mama nahigugma kanimo." Si Sandra miignon.

"Dili."

"Nakita ko ikaw uban kaniya kagahapon, ang adlaw wala , ang adlaw?" Si Sandra miingon.

"Dili, mao kana ikaw." Gibalda ni Jenny.

"Mag-uban?" Si Sandra nangutana.

"Magkauban." Si Jenny mitubag.

"Amahan, inahan, igsoon, tanan nahigugma kanimo." Si Sandra miingon.

"Bueno, nga gipasigarbo nimo, ako kinahanglan moingon." Si Jenny miingon.

"Ngano?" Si Sandra nangutana.

"Nga gihigugma nimo ang imong kaugalingon." Si Jenny mitubag.

"Dili ako mapahitas-on." Nagprotesta si Sandra.

"Unsa ang gugma kanimo?" Si Jenny nangutana.

"Ang tanan." Si Sandra mitubag.

"Suginli ako unsay wala nako mahibaloi." Si Jenny miingon. "Kinahanglan kong moadto."

"Dili ko gusto nga mawala kanimo." Si Sandra miinsistir.

"Giatiman nimo ang imong kaugalingon." Si Jenny miingon.

"Dili, gusto kong mag-atiman kanimo." Si Sandra miinsistir.

Panahon 20:00

"Mas madanihon ka paglaum, apan imo akong gihimo nga makalolooy. Unsay mahitabo nako?" Si Mark nangutana.

"Wala ako masayud." Si Jenny mitubag.

"Nganong nahadlok kaayo kita nga magkinabuhi nga walay kabalaka? bata ko, ang pangunang kabalaka mao ang kagawasan, karon kini gugma. Tungod ang gugma mao ang kanser bag-ong henerasyon ang mga stem cell mao ako, ako, akong kaugalingon. Ang una nga balak gugma gisulat Latin, usa ka pinulongan nga patay, busa ang gugma iya mga patay. Ang gugma materyal nga mga butang mao ang akong gipasabut; kini nagpalambo kasakit. Aron makabaton o dili. Ang usa ka lalaki nga nag-ilis nga nagsul-ob ingon nga usa ka babaye nga nagpakasal usa ka tawo nga nagsul-ob ingon nga usa ka lalaki; kini nahitabo kagahapon, nakita ko kini kaugalingon kong mga mata. Ako tigulang , kinahanglan nga pasayloon mo ako. Ang maong kahadlok tawo, nahadlok nga mag-inusara. Ang akong balay wala balay, kini usa ka dapit negosyo, usa ka dapit negosasyon, akong kaugalingon nga Davos, karon usa ka kumpisalan." Gipasabut ni Mark.

"Gihigugma mo ba ako?" Si Jenny nangutana.

"Tan-awa ang akong nawong." Si Mark mitubag. "Wala koy interes bisan unsa niining higayona. Wala ko'y interes alang akong pamilya. Wala'y bisan unsa nga kahaw-ang akong kinabuhi; apan karon nga ikaw ania dinhi, ako adunay katarungan nga mabuhi pag-usab. Ako adunay usa ka makahahadlok nga tahas nga una kanako. Kadto usa ka walay sulod nga dalan bakak nga mga ideya. Imong gipuno ang akong kinabuhi. Apan karon nga gibiyaan mo ako, imong gilaglag ang tanan. Nahadlok kaayo ko nga mawala ka. Nahadlok kaayo ko nga ako masakit pag-usab. Mianhi ka nga usa ka mesiyas aron paglaglag tanan karon ikaw makahimo pagsinggit nga fait accompli." Si Mark miingon.

"De rien. Dili kanunay nga usa ka katuyoan

kinabuhi. Nakita ba nimo si Mela? Nagkinahanglan ko og tabang." Si Jenny nangutana.

"Mibiya siya balay nga sayo kaayo buntag. Gidala niya ang kamera imong mga hulagway niini." Si Mark mitubag.

"Asa siya?" Si Jenny nangutana.

"Panimalay, balik uban iyang mga ginikanan. Siya mibilin alang kanimo, ang sabon nga solusyon bula, ang iyang espesyal nga resipe; Gusto niya nga itago nimo kini imong bulsa." Si Mark miingon.

"Akong buhaton. Karon tugutan ko ikaw nga mobalik mga kalihokan imong pamilya." Si Jenny miingon.

"Dili, ulahi kaayo. Imposible nga ibalik ang bisan unsang kredibilidad niining puntoha." Gipsabut ni Mark. Walay bisan unsa nga bahin kanako; wala'y bisan unsa nga rason alang ingon nga pagsulay unang dapit. Buot kong makamata gikan niining makalilisang nga damgo. Ang akong gusto hingpit nga lahi, hingpit nga talagsaon, hingpit nga tinuod. Tingali ang pipila ka mga tawo walay hingpit nga talento paghimo og maayong mga pagpili. Nakuha nako ang pipila ka mga shortcut mao kini ang akong naangkon. Ako nanghinaut nga ako makasugod pag-usab, isip usa ka bag-ong natawo, apan nahadlok ako nga wala ako'y daghang oras."

"Mark, ikaw adunay daghang panahon." Si Jenny miingon.

"Dili, ang kamatuoran mao ang makapasubo nga kamatuoran; Dili ako yuta, dili ako adlaw, wala ako langit, dili ako bulan; Daghan kaayo ko dili kaayo talagsaon, dili nako angayng kabuang ang akong kaugalingon ang mga naglibot kanako. Ang kalayo, tubig hangin adunay katuyoan usa ka ideya kung asa moadto; Dili ko." Si Mark miingon.

"Bueno, tingali kami anaa mao ra nga sakayan." Si Jenny miingon.

Let's Compare

Bahin 1

GABUN, SMOG, SINGGIT sa mga tawo; ang bugtong butang nga naa sa akong hunahuna mao ang kalibog. Pagkalibog alang sa mga butang nga walay kahulogan. Gihunahuna sa Dios ang mga tawo, ug gisultihan sila sa paglakaw ngadto sa disyerto. Didto siya, nagtindog didto. Ang kabukiran ug disyerto nagsunod sa pagkalapad niining komplikado nga yuta nga gipamulak sa pagkawalay kaluoy sa bulkan, ug sa akong mga kalihokan, nga hapit na mapalayo alang sa maayo--unta.

Nagdrayb ko, oo, layo sa tanang butang nga akong gitukod, ang tanan nga akong naangkon, mga butang nga walay kahulong.

Ang mga zebra (marka sa trapiko) hapsay nga gipintalan, mga nanambong nga mitabok, mga simbolo sa trapiko nga nagpagrabe sa kinabuhi; sa pagluwas sa katawhan uban sa mga semiotics? Tingali usa kini ka pagbati. Ang kakulangan sa kagawasan.

Ang mga estudyante milaktaw sa klase, ang bintana sa sakyanan gipaubos, sama sa kanunay, ang hangin mahinungdanon; Huwebes na, sila nagsaulog. Pagsaulog nila sa unsa? Unsa gayud ang kalainan tali sa mga singgit sa mga tawo ug sa mga singgit sa mga mananap?

Tingali dili sila mga estudyante, gibalibaran nila ang mga hairdos ug nagsul-ob sila ug mga kupo. Ang usa nagalabay sa iyang kupo sa hangin, siya adunay epileptic nga dagway, ug siya nagdagan aron sa pagsugat sa usa ka babaye, lain nga itom ug puti nga talan-awon, laing konsepto sa gugma nga dili matukib, oo sila sa pagkatinuod mga apan kini nagsamok kanako sa usa ka gamay; Siguradong pamilyar na siya nako-dili siya. Kinsa siya? Kini usa ka ting-ulan nga adlaw, o dili; tingali nag-ulan lang usa ka oras sa wala pa, tingali kini ulan usa ka gatus ka tuig na ang milabay.

Ako sa panihapon uban sa akong pamilya, sa katapusan. Ang sulugoon naghatag kanako sa sulat; Usa lang kini ka pahina, tulo ka mga pulong: Moabot ako ugma. Kon wala pa nimo makilala si Jenny kaniadto, pasidan? Siya makalignaw kaayo. Siya adunay tulo ka mga pagbati: Ducatis, hilig, ug psychoanalysis. Ang katapusan nga usa mao ang usa ka gamay sa annoyance ug kadaghanan sa mga kalag nga magpalayo gikan sa iyang tungod niana nga hinungdan. Kini usa ka misteryo alang kanako kung giunsa siya adunay usa sa labing makapaikag nga pagkinabuhi alang sa usa ka babaye sa iyang edad. Uban sa usa ka makalingaw nga tête-à-tête, ug daghan nga marmol, siya nakahimo sa pagtukod sa usa ka talagsaon nga Tuscan-style nga villa uban sa sulud sa gawas ug sa mga olympic swimming pool sa usa sa labing inila nga kasilinganan sa La Jolla, California.

Makaiikag, siya dili gayud sa balay. Nagdrayb siya sa iyang Ducati nga adunay tambok nga pitaka sa likod sa iyang pantalon. Sa akong kahibalo, wala siyay bisan unsang pitaka ug iyang gitamay ang mga aksesorya sa batang babaye. Uban sa iyang foppish nga reputasyon iyang nakabungkag daghang mga kasingkasing, ug pipila ka mga bukog usab; siya walay hingpit nga interes alang sa usa ka makanunayon nga relasyon, ug ngadto kaniya, ang gugma nga mga kauban mao lamang ang makalingaw.

Busa, unsa karon? Ang sulud nga babaye nagtutok kang Jenny nga anaa sa tanaman nagbasa sa usa ka makalilisang nga basahon; Wala pa ako makakita sa iyang pagbasa kaniadto, gawas nga dili ko maghunahuna nga ang ingon nga genre nahisubay sa iyang dautan nga intelihensya. Ngano nga siya motutok kaniya sama niana, aduna bay butang alang sa usag usa, usa ka butang nga wala nako mahibaloi? Nagatindog siya sa mga kahoy, unsay iyang gibuhat? Nagtan-aw sa mga pantalon ni Jenny?

Tingali ang pagtan-aw ni Mela sa libro nga Jenny naghupot ug wala gani magbasa. Dili, dili OK nga usbon ang hilisgutan.

Hikalimti kini, naningkamot siya nga makuha ang iyang pagtagad; dili, si Jenny naningkamot sa pagkuha sa iyang pagtagad, oh dili, wala gyud siya nagsalikway kaniya karon. Maayo siya. Siya natugaw, karon siya mikalagiw nga wala diha sa sulod sa balay, dili siya maayo nga magdadagan, dili siya maayo sa daghang mga butang. Anaa siya sa atubangan sa usa ka salamin, pagtuon sa mga postura, pagdayeg sa iyang kaugalingon; Gikuha niya ang usa ka ariyos, karon iyang giwagtang ang laing usa. Siya dili matagbaw; siya ang nagbutang kanila balik. Ang iyang mga ngabil, oo iyang gihikap ang iyang mga ngabil; sila mga manipis, lawasnon. Wala pa siya pahiyom. Dan, siya na balik sa tanaman, naglakaw siya sa sagbut sama sa usa ka baliw, siya naghuyop sa usa ka sungkod; usa ka bag-ong double bubble nga teorya? Wala siya mahibalo kung unsa ang impyerno nga iyang gihunahuna. Siya adunay tan-aw sa iyang nawong, naghilak siya, nagtan-aw na usab siya kang Jenny, kinsa nahibal-an, tingali siya nahimo uban kaniya. Nagdagan siya sa sulod sa balay uban sa kabuang, siya anaa sa kusina, ang gas hose, iyang gibira ang gas hose gikan sa stove ug gibutang kini sa iyang baba. Naghimo siya og pipila ka aerosol, apan adunay problema nga pagginhawa. Siya buang, oh Dios, siya gayud buang, nahimo niya kini kaniadto. Ako adunay pagbati nga gusto niya nga patyon ang iyang kaugalingon. OK, naa siya sa salog, apan si Jenny matud pa, sa akong hunahuna siya nagtan-aw niini nga sine kaniadto; Nagdalagan siya sa sulod, gipili siya niya sama sa usa ka rag nga monyeka; Giguyod niya siya ngadto sa kwarto.

"Hoy, ikaw ba ang tanan?" Nangutana siya.

Siya naglingolingo sa iyang ulo sa pipila ka mga higayon; nahibal-an niya kung unsaon kini buhaton. Talagsaon siya. Siya nagatutok kaniya; siya natunaw.

Dili siya makasulti og usa ka pulong, nagbag-o siya sa iyang hunahuna.

"Oo, tanan, tanan." Si Mela mitubag.

"Tinuod?" Si Jenny nangutana.

"Oo." Si Mela mitubag.

"Gihatagan mo ako ug kalisang." Si Jenny miingon.

"Dili, wala ako." Si Mela mitubag.

"Nganong gibuhat nimo kana?" Si Jenny nangutana.

"Tungod kay usa ka tawo ang gusto sa akong utok." Si Mela mitubag.

"Kinsa?" Si Jenny nangutana.

"Usa ka higala." Si Mela mitubag.

"Komosta ako?" Si Jenny nangutana.

"Ikaw usab." Si Mela mitubag.

"Ikaw buang!" Si Jenny miingon.

"Numero uno ba ako? Si Mela nangutana.

Iyang gipahigda siya sa iyang higdaanan, usa ka babaye. Si Mela nagbira sa sinina, unsay iyang gibuhat? Gidapit ba siya niya?

Dili, dili siya interesado. Dili siya malipayon, wala siya makasabut sa usa ka butang. Siya nag-ayo sa iyang sinina, gipatapik niya ang iyang buhok, naghilak siya, gihagkan niya ang iyang kamot; Oh Dios ko, siya gayud ang misulod niini. Ang mga mata ni Jenny dako, gamhanan. Gipaduol niya kini. OK, naa na siya sa ibabaw niya, naluoy ba siya alang niya? Nag-agi sila sa usa ka gamay, siya nagpadayon sa pagpugong batok sa iyang crotch, nahibal-an niya kung unsaon kini buhaton.

Karon siya malipayon.

?

Nagahigda ako. Dili ako, dili, ug ako nagsul-ob og pajama; dili kini iya. Aw, mangatulog na usab kita. Dili ko. Buweno, niining higayona ako mahimo usab nga maglakaw sa gawas ug makaginhawa sa presko nga hangin, sans veils; oh oo, kaadlawon kaayo, apan kung wala pa nimo nakit-an, nagtuo ako nga nagkagrabe. Ngano? Wala ako masayud. Kini mahitabo kanatong tanan usahay sa kinabuhi. Makahahadlok kini; Namatikdan nako nga duha ka mga babaye ang natulog sa usa ka higdaanan sa lawak sa sala. Jenny, ang Ducati nga babaye; Dili ako sigurado kung kinsa ang usa; Sandra, akong primogeniture. Dili ko tugutan ang mga kalihokan sa homosexual sulod sa akong balay, dili kini ang pulo sa Sappho; Manghinaut ako nga wala ako'y hunahuna ug dili makakita, tingali natulog pa ko. Buweno, mangatulog kita balik, si Anna wala makamatikod sa usa ka butang, maayo alang kaniya; dili siya kinahanglan nga makakita kanako sa ingon nga kahimtang.

Kini opisyal, ako nasakit, ako usa ka tawong masakiton. Ug si Sandra, ang akong anak nga babaye sunod kanako samtang ako naghigda. Ang akong lawas dili masakiton, apan ang akong hunahuna mao. Dili kini makita ni Sandra; Si Jenny naglakaw lang ug siya nagtutok kanako, ang iyang pahiyom nagsulti kanako sa usa ka butang. Tingali ako kinahanglan nga mangutana kaniya. Alang sa mga rekord, si Jenny usa ko ka estudyante, usa ka talagsaon nga usa ka tawo sa dihang ako usa ka puli nga magtutudlo. Gikuha niya ang habol ug gihatagan niya ako og usa ka tiil sa pagmasahe; Si Sandra wala pa gisulti sa usa ka pulong, apan iyang gisundan ang mga lihok ni Jenny uban sa iyang maalamon nga mga mata; Kinahanglan nga sila magkahiusa; ang akong anak nga lalaki nga si Mark nakapaamgo kanako niana. Gipataas ni Jenny ang akong mga bitiis; Nakita nako nga kini usa ka matang sa rejuvenating therapy nga iyang nakat-unan sa Europe uban sa iyang gang sa motorsiklo. Aw, sa usa ka paagi, maayo ang akong gibati.

Oo, usa na ka semana karon, ug ako nagsugod na sa pagbati nga mas maayo, hapit laing lalaki. Ang tawo nga gusto nakong mahimo; Dili, tingali dili pa, wala pa. Adunay usa pa ka kaaway sa sulod nako, kinsa man?

Oh oo, usa ka biyahe ngadto sa nasud; Nagdrayb si Jenny sama sa usa ka baliw, nahigugma siya sa iyang

Ducati; apan niining higayona ako kinahanglan gayud nga mosulti kaniya unsa ang nahitabo, kini usa ka moral nga butang. Oo, gisultihan ko siya nga adunay kalibog sa akong hunahuna sa takna ug kinahanglan ko nga makuha kini gikan sa akong dughan. Wala pa ko makasulti og usa ka pulong, apan siya malipayon, ug kana nakapalipay kanako; pamahaw ug pagsakay sa lanaw, ingon og usa ka maayong ideya.

"Suginli ako Jenny, unsay among gikaon?" Nangutana ko.

"Dili ako ang gigutom, apan ako magabantay kanimo; kanunay ka nga makalingaw uban sa kutsilyo ug sa kakha sa imong mga kamot; Makakuha ako'g inspirasyon sa pagpamalandong sa imong mga pagduhaduha." Si Jenny mitubag.

"Naa ba ako sa kasamok?" Nangutana ko.

"Wala ako masayud. Anaa ka ba sa kasamok?" Si Jenny mitubag.

"Nawad-an ka sa dula." Miingon ko.

"Ganahan ko sa imong mga pulong." Si Jenny miingon.

"Ganahan ko sa imong buhok." Miingon ko.

Sige, pamahaw na, karon na gyud ang panahon sa pagsulti kaniya unsa ang problema. Siya nagdagan, siya kusog; siya tulin nga paspas, diin ang impyerno nagdagan siya? OK, nakit-an ko siya; siya nahugno sa yuta ug siya nagtutok sa kalangitan; Kanunay niya kanang buhaton sa tanaman sa campus.

Mm, kinahanglan nga mao ra nga libro. Suginli ako Jenny, unsay imong gibasa?

"Gihaylo mo ako, imo akong gipanag-iya, miabot ka, ug ikaw nakadaug. Karon kinahanglan kong tawagon ang akong kaugalingon nga usa ka butang nga pagyubit. Ang akong suod nga mga higala nakasaksi sa akong pagkapukan." Siya nagbasa.

"Kinsa ang nagsulat niana?" Nangutana ko.

"Ang mga pulong mas importante kay sa magsusulat. Kinahanglan nga hubaron sa magbabasa ang mga pulong nga gusto niya. Kini usa ka moral nga butang." Si Jenny miingon.

"Sa akong hunahuna wala ang ingon nga mga pulong gisulat alang sa usa ka partikular nga rason gawas—" Gipasabut ko.

"Gawas?" Si Jenny mitubag.

"Kalimti kini." Miingon ko.

"Husto ka; Wala nako mabasa ang mga pulong aron pagsulti kanimo sa kamatuoran." Si Jenny miignon.

“Mangadto ta sa balay.” Miingon ko.

?

Ang postman nahibalik, nakahatag siya og laing sulat ngadto kang Mela, ang sulugoon. Gihatag lang niya kini kanako; Kinahanglan nga kini usa pa ka bon vivant ugma, kinsay mahimo? Walay usa nga moabot; wala kini gitumong kanako.”

“Jenny, kini alang nimo.” Miingon ko.

Gitan-aw ni Jenny ang sulat.

“OK, kinahanglan kong mobiya ugma.” Siya miingon.

Bahin 2

Panahon:17:00

"Jenny, dili ka kinahanglan nga mobiya." Si Anna miingon.

"Nahadlok ko nga kinahanglan ko." Si Jenny mitubag.

"Dili, dili ko nimo tugutan." Miinsistir si Anna.

"Usa ka adlaw o duha, unsa man ang kalainan?" Si Jenny nangutana.

"Sukad nga ikaw miabot sa niini nga balay ang tanan nausab, ako nausab, imong giablihan?" Gipatin-aw ni Anna.

"Anna, hunong, palihug." Si Jenny miingon.

"Dili, mao kini kung unsa kini; Nakaamgo ko karon nga ang akong bana dili gayud ang tawo nga akong gihigugma ug?" Si Anna miingon.

"Dili, wala ako moanhi tungod niana nga hinungdan." Gibalda ni Jenny.

"Kinahanglan nga paminawon mo ako." Si Anna miingon.

“Unsa ang iyang mga sayup?” Si Jenny nangutana.

“Sa akong hunahuna ang iyang mga sayop mao ang akong sayop.” Si Anna mitubag.

“Niini nga kahimtang wala ka'y problema.” Gipatin-aw ni Jenny.

“Ako buang.” Si Anna miingon.

“Dili, kinahanglan nga dili ka.” Si Jenny miingon.

“Gidumtan nako ang akong kaugalingon ug ang tanan nga naglibut kanako.” Si Anna miingon.

“Dili, dili kinahanglan.” Si Jenny miingon.

“Naghunahuna ba kamo nga ako iya sa kalibutan?” Si Anna nangutana.

“Maayo kini nga pangutana.” Si Jenny mitubag.

“Naghunahuna ka ba nga makapabilin ka og gamay pa?” Si Anna nangutana.

“Ngano?” Si Jenny nangutana.

“Dili ko gustong mamatay nga wala nimo.” Si Anna mitubag.

“Ikaw mabuhi hangtud sa kahangturan.” Si Jenny miingon.

“Sa unsang paagi ka makasiguro?” Si Anna nangutana.

Aduna ka'y aura sa kaalam, usa ka aura sa tinguha, ug gipanalanginan ka sa taas nga kinabuhi.” Si Jenny mitubag.

“Nagahatag ka ba kanako og usa ka pagbasa? Ikaw usa ka babaye nga daghang mga talento, apan ako nagduhaduha mahitungod niining butang nga aura, dili ko kini makita.” Si Anna miingon.

“Ang imong aura usa ka butang nga dili nimo makita, apan ang uban sa imong palibot.” Gipatin-aw ni Jenny.

Panahon 18:00

“Utang ko kanimo ang kalibutan. Ang tanan nga imo ginhatag sa akon. Karon nagtuo ko nga ang kinabuhi adunay kahulugan. Naghunahuna ako nga gidumtan nako ang mga babaye, tungod kay gidumtan nako ang akong inahan. Karon ang tanan lahi, Jenny, ang tanan klaro kaayo. Ang tanan?” Si Mark miingon.

“Ang tanan maayo, Mark; ang tanan maayo. Ang imong inahan nahigugma kanimo. Sila nahigugma kanimo dinhi niining balaya.” Si Jenny miingon.

“Ug gihigugma ko ikaw. Akong buhaton.” Si Mark miingon.

“Ug ako nahigugma usab kanimo, apan kinahanglan nimo nga masabtan.” Si Jenny miingon.

“Dili, dili ko tugutan nga makasabut, ang akong kasingkasing dili motugot kanako.” Si Mark miingon.

“Adunay usa ka bag-ong sakit sa tibuok kalibutan.” Gipatin-aw ni Jenny.

“Pakigsulti kanako, unsa man kini?” Si Mark nangutana.

“Nahadlok ka ba sa gugma?” Si Jenny nangutana.

“Nahadlok ko nga magul-anon kaayo.” Si Mark mitubag.

“Niini nga kaso ang usa ka estatuwa mao ang tubag?” Si Jenny miingon.
“Ang imong estatuwa, ang Ducati girl nga estatuwa, akong simbahon kini ingon nga diyosa, diha mismo sa akong kwarto, apan nahadlok ko nga ang usa ka estatuwa mahimong magpasabut sa katapusan sa kinabuhi.” Si Mark mitubag.

“Ingna ko; unsa ang akong sayop, nga ania dinhi?” Si Mark nangutana.

Panahon 19:00

"Wala ko mahibal-an ang gugma sa wala pa nako gigahin kining talagsaon nga mga hapon kauban nimo. Ang tanan nahigugma kanimo, ang akong mga higala dili makahunong nga makig-istorya kanimo ug dili ako makatulog nga dili maghunahuna kanimo. Unsay imong gibuhat nako?" Si Sandra nangutana.

"Unsa man ang akong nahimo kanimo, Sandra?" Si Jenny nangutana.

"Ikaw ang una nga naghisgot mahitungod sa gugma. Sa usa ka paagi, gipahayag mo ang giyera sa akong kalag." Si Sanda mitubag.

"Uh, nga kinahanglan nga makahadlok." Si Jenny miingon.

"Sa sinugdan, apan karon nga nakaila na ko nimo, dili na ko mahadlok." Si Sandra miingon.

"Ang akong tingali mao ang pagpakita kanimo sa dalan." Si Jenny miingon.

"Ug ang kapalaran, unsa ang akong padulngan kon wala ka? Unsa ang gugma, laing matang sa kanser nga walay tambal? Ingna ko." Si Sandra nangutana.

"Kinahanglan kong moadto." Si Jenny miingon.

"Dili, ayaw ko biya-i!" Misinggit si Sandra.

“Ihatag ko kanimo ang usa ka kopa nga kape.” Si Jenny miingon.

“Dili, palihug paminawa ako.” Si Sandra miingon.

“Kinahanglan nga magsul-ob ka sa dili pa magbagtok ang imong inahan sa pultahan.” Gitambagan ni Jenny.

“Si Mama nahigugma kanimo.” Si Sandra miignon.

“Dili.”

“Nakita ko ikaw uban kaniya kagahapon, ug ang adlaw sa wala pa, ug ang adlaw?” Si Sandra miingon.

“Dili, mao kana ikaw.” Gibalda ni Jenny.

“Mag-uban?” Si Sandra nangutana.

“Magkauban.” Si Jenny mitubag.

“Amahan, inahan, igsoon, tanan nahigugma kanimo.” Si Sandra miingon.

“Bueno, nga gipasigarbo nimo, ako kinahanglan moingon.” Si Jenny miingon.

“Ngano?” Si Sandra nangutana.

"Nga gihigugma nimo ang imong kaugalingon." Si Jenny mitubag.

"Dili ako mapahitas-on." Nagprotesta si Sandra.

"Unsa ang gugma kanimo?" Si Jenny nangutana.

"Ang tanan." Si Sandra mitubag.

"Suginli ako unsay wala nako mahibaloi." Si Jenny miingon. "Kinahanglan kong moadto."

"Dili ko gusto nga mawala kanimo." Si Sandra miinsistir.

"Giatiman nimo ang imong kaugalingon." Si Jenny miingon.

"Dili, gusto kong mag-atiman kanimo." Si Sandra miinsistir.

Panahon 20:00

"Mas madanihon ka kay sa paglaum, apan imo akong gihimo nga makalolooy. Unsay mahitabo nako?" Si Mark nangutana.

"Wala ako masayud." Si Jenny mitubag.

"Nganong nahadlok kaayo kita nga magkinabuhi nga walay kabalaka? Sa bata pa ko, ang pangunang kabalaka mao ang kagawasan, karon kini gugma. Tungod kay ang gugma mao ang kanser sa bag-ong henerasyon ug ang mga stem cell mao ako, ako, ug akong kaugalingon. Ang una nga balak sa gugma gisulat sa Latin, usa ka pinulongan nga patay, busa ang gugma iya sa mga patay. Ang gugma sa materyal nga mga butang mao ang akong gipasabut; kini nagpalambo sa kasakit. Aron makabaton o dili. Ang usa ka lalaki nga nag-ilis nga nagsul-ob ingon nga usa ka babaye nga nagpakasal sa usa ka tawo nga nagsul-ob ingon nga usa ka lalaki; kini nahitabo kagahapon, nakita ko kini sa kaugalingon kong mga mata. Ako tigulang na, kinahanglan nga pasayloon mo ako. Ang maong kahadlok sa tawo, nahadlok nga mag-inusara. Ang akong balay wala na sa balay, kini usa ka dapit sa negosyo, usa ka dapit sa negosasyon, akong kaugalingon nga Davos, ug karon usa ka kumpisalan." Gipasabut ni Mark.

"Gihigugma mo ba ako?" Si Jenny nangutana.

"Tan-awa ang akong nawong." Si Mark mitubag. "Wala koy interes sa bisan unsa niining higayona. Wala na ko'y interes alang sa akong pamilya. Wala'y bisan unsa nga kahaw-ang sa akong kinabuhi; apan karon nga ikaw ania dinhi, ako adunay katarungan nga mabuhi pag-usab. Ako adunay usa ka makahahadlok nga tahas nga una kanako. Kadto usa ka walay sulod nga dalan sa bakak nga mga ideya. Imong gipuno ang akong kinabuhi. Apan karon nga gibiyaan mo ako, imong gilaglag ang tanan. Nahadlok kaayo ko nga mawala ka. Nahadlok kaayo ko nga ako masakit pag-usab. Mianhi ka nga usa ka mesiyas aron sa paglaglag sa tanan ug karon ikaw makahimo sa pagsinggit nga fait accompli." Si Mark miingon.

"De rien. Dili kanunay nga usa ka katuyoan sa kinabuhi. Nakita ba nimo si Mela? Nagkinahanglan ko og tabang." Si Jenny nangutana.

"Mibiya siya sa balay nga sayo kaayo sa buntag. Gidala niya ang kamera sa imong mga hulagway niini." Si Mark mitubag.

"Asa man siya?" Si Jenny nangutana.

"Panimalay, balik uban sa iyang mga ginikanan. Siya mibilin alang kanimo, ang sabon nga solusyon sa bula, ang iyang espesyal nga resipe; Gusto niya nga itago nimo kini sa imong bulsa." Si Mark miingon.

"Akong buhaton. Karon tugutan ko ikaw nga mobalik sa mga kalihokan sa imong pamilya." Si Jenny miingon.

"Dili, ulahi na kaayo. Imposible nga ibalik ang bisan unsang kredibilidad niining puntoha." Gipsabut ni Mark. Walay bisan unsa nga bahin kanako; wala'y bisan unsa nga rason alang sa ingon nga pagsulay sa unang dapit. Buot kong makamata gikan niining makalilisang nga damgo. Ang akong gusto hingpit nga lahi, hingpit nga talagsaon, hingpit nga tinuod. Tingali ang pipila ka mga tawo walay hingpit nga talento sa paghimo og maayong mga pagpili. Nakuha nako ang pipila ka mga shortcut ug mao kini ang akong naangkon. Ako nanghinaut nga ako makasugod pag-usab, isip usa ka bag-ong natawo, apan nahadlok ako nga wala na ako'y daghang oras."

"Mark, ikaw adunay daghang panahon." Si Jenny miingon.

"Dili, ang kamatuoran mao ang makapasubo nga kamatuoran; Dili ako yuta, dili ako adlaw, wala ako langit, ug dili ako bulan; Daghan kaayo ko ug dili kaayo talagsaon, dili na nako angayng kabuang ang akong kaugalingon ug ang mga naglibot kanako. Ang kalayo, tubig ug hangin adunay katuyoan ug usa ka ideya kung asa moadto; Dili ko." Si Mark miingon.

"Bueno, tingali kami anaa sa mao ra nga sakayan." Si Jenny miingon.

Challenge Translation

Part 1

FOG, SMOG, CRIES of humans; the only thing I have in my mind is confusion. Confusion for things that are meaningless. God made people think, and told them to take a walk into the desert. There he was, standing there. Mountains and desert following the curvature of this complicated earth carbonized by volcanic discontent, and my affairs, which are about to be tossed away for good?I hope so. I'm driving away, yes, away from everything I've built, everything I possess, negligible things. Zebras neatly painted, pedestrians crossing, traffic symbols exacerbating life; saving humanity with semiotics? Perhaps it's just a feeling. Freedom deprivation. Students skipping class, my car window is rolled down, as always, air is vital; it's Thursday, they're celebrating. Celebrating what? What really is the difference between the cries of humans and the cries of animals? Perhaps they're not students, they have disturbing hairdos and they're wearing trench coats. One is throwing his coat up in the air, he has an epileptic look, and he's running to meet a girl, another black and white scene, another obscure love concept, yeah, they must be students, but it's bothering me a little; she's definitely familiar to me?he isn't. Who is he? It's a rainy day, or it isn't;

maybe it just rained an hour before, maybe it's rain of one hundred years ago.

I'm at dinner with my family, finally. The maid hands me the mail; it's only one page, three words: I shall arrive tomorrow. If you haven't met Jenny before, I shall warn you?she's an incredible piece of work. She has three passions: Ducatis, seduction, and psychoanalysis. The last one is a bit of an annoyance and most souls stay away from her for that reason. It's quite a mystery to me how she has one of the most interesting lifestyle for a girl of her age. With engaging tête–à–tête, and plenty of marble, she managed to build a lavish Tuscan-style villa with indoor and outdoor Olympic-length swimming pools in one of the most prestigious neighborhood of La Jolla. Interestingly, she's never home. She travels on her Ducati with a fat wallet right in the back of her pants. To my knowledge, she doesn't own any purse and she despises girls' accessories. With her foppish reputation she managed to break many hearts, and a few bones too; she has no absolute interest for a steady relationship, and to her, love partners are just recreational.

So, now what? The maid is staring at Jenny, who is in the garden reading an atrocious book; I've never seen her reading before, besides I wouldn't think such genre would be consistent with her sinister intelligentsia. Why would she stare at her like that, do they have a thing for each other, something that I don't know? She's standing by the trees, what is she doing? Staring at Jenny's pants? Jenny always spreads her legs when she's sitting; her treasure is somehow prominent, inviting, but never disturbing to the eye. Perhaps Mela's staring at the book Jenny is holding and not even reading. No, it isn't OK to change the subject. Forget it, she's trying to get her attention?no?Jenny is trying to get her attention, oh no, she's really ignoring her now. She's good. She's disturbed, now she's running away awkwardly inside the house, she's not a good runner, she's not good at a lot of things. She's in front of a mirror, studying postures, admiring herself; she's removing one earring, now she's removing the other one. She's not satisfied; she's putting them back on. Her lips, yes, she's touching her lips; they are thin, carnal. She hasn't cracked a smile yet. Well, she's back in the garden, she's walking onto the grass like a madwoman, she's blowing on a stick; a new double bubble conjecture? She doesn't know what the hell she's thinking. She has a bland look on her face, she's weeping, she's staring at Jenny again, who knows, maybe she's done with her. She's running inside the house with madness, she's in the kitchen?the gas hose?she pulled out the gas hose from the stove and she's putting it in her mouth. She's doing some aerosol but she has problem breathing. She's crazy, oh God, she's really crazy, she has done this before. I have the feeling she made an attempt to take her life. OK, she's on the floor, but Jenny is sharp, I think she watched this movie before; she's running inside, she's picking her up like a rag doll; she's dragging her into the bedroom.

“Hey you, everything's all right?” She asks.

She shakes her head a few times; she knows how to do that, apparently. She's dramatic, sort of. She's looking at her; she's melting.

She can't say a word, she changes her mind.

"Yep, everything-everything."
"For real?"
"Yep."
"You gave me a fright."
"No, I did not."
"Why did you do that?"
"Because it wanted my brain."
"Who?"
"A friend."
"What about me?"
"You too."
"Silly."
"Am I great?"

She laid her on her bed, what a girl. Mela is pulling the dress up, what is she doing? Is she inviting her in?

No, she's not that interested. She's not happy, she doesn't understand a thing. She's fixing her dress, she's fixing her hair, she's weeping, she's kissing her hand; oh my God, she's really into it. Jenny's eyes are big, powerful. She's pulling her closer. OK, she's on top of her now, is she feeling sorry for her? They're moving a little, she's pressing hard against her crotch, she knows how to do that.

Now she's happy.

?

I'm in bed; no, I'm not, and I'm wearing a pajama; it doesn't even belong to me. Well, let's go to sleep again. No, I cannot. Well, in this case I might as well walk outside and breathe some fresh air, sans veils; oh yes, dawn is so pretty, but just in case you haven't noticed yet, I believe I'm deteriorating. Why? I don't know. It happens to all of us sometime in life. It's disturbing; I just noticed that two women are sleeping in the same bed in the guestroom. Jenny, the Ducati girl; I'm not quite sure who the other one might be; Sandra, my primogeniture. I wouldn't tolerate homosexual activities inside my house, this isn't the isle of Sappho; I hope I'm just out of my mind and can't see clear, perhaps I'm still asleep. Well, let's head back to bed, Anna hasn't noticed a thing, good for her; she shouldn't see me in such a state.

It's official, I am sick, I'm a sick man. And Sandra, my daughter is next to me while I lay in bed. My body isn't actually diseased, but my mind is. Sandra can't see that; Jenny just walked in and she's staring at me, her smile is telling me something. Perhaps I should ask her. For the records, Jenny was a student of mine, a rather unusual one back when I was a substitute teacher. She's removing the blanket and she's giving me a foot massage; Sandra hasn't mumbled a word yet, but she's following Jenny's moves with her smart eyes; it's imperative they have a thing together; my son Mark made me well aware of that. Jenny is stretching my legs; I can see it's some sort of rejuvenating therapy she has learned in Europe with her motorcycle gang. Well, in a way, I feel good.

Yes, it's been a week now, and I'm truly starting to feel better, almost another man. The man I always wanted to be; no, perhaps not quite, not yet. There's still an enemy inside me, who could that be?

Oh yes, a ride to the country; Jenny is driving like a maniac, she loves her Ducati; but at this point I really need to tell her what's going on, it's a moral thing. Yes, I just told her that there's confusion in my mind at the moment and I need to get it out of my chest. I've yet to say a word but she's happy, and that makes me happy; breakfast and a ride to the lake, it seems like a good idea.

"Tell me Jenny, what are we eating?"

"I'm not that hungry, but I shall watch you; you're always fascinating with knife and fork in your hands; I shall get some inspiration for contemplating on your doubts."

"Am I in trouble?"

"I don't know. Are you in trouble?"

"You lost the game."

"I love your words."

"I love your hair."

All right, breakfast is over, now it's really time to tell her what the problem is. She's running, she's fast; she's really fast, where the hell is she running to? OK, I found her; she just collapsed on the ground and she's staring at the sky; she used to do that quite often in the campus garden.

Mm, must be the same book.

"Tell me Jenny, what are you reading?"

"You seduced me, you possessed me, you came, and you prevailed. I should now call myself a subject of scorn. My close friends have witnessed my fall."

"Who wrote that? I asked."

"The words are more important than the writer. The reader must interpret the words as she likes. It's a moral thing."

"I don't think such words were written for any particular reason except?"

"Except?"

"Forget it."

"You're right; I haven't read the words to tell you the truth."

"Let's head back home."

?

The postman is back, he has delivered another letter to Mela, the maid. She just handed it to me; it must be another bon vivant arriving tomorrow, who might be? No one is coming; it isn't even addressed to me.

"Jenny, this is for you," I gestured.

"OK, I must leave tomorrow," she says.

Part 2

Time 17:00

"Jenny, you must not leave."
"I'm afraid I have to."
"No, I won't let you."
"A day or two, what difference would make?"
"Since you came into this house everything has changed, I have changed, you have opened?"
"Anna, stop, please."
"No, it is what it is; I now realized that my husband isn't really the man I love, and?"
"No, I didn't come here for that reason."
"You must listen to me."
"What are his faults?"
"I think his faults are my faults."
"In this case you don't have a problem."
"I'm mad."
"No, you shouldn't be."
"I hate myself and everything around me."
"No, you shouldn't."
"Do you think that I belong to this world?"
"It's a good question."
"Do you think you can stay a little bit longer?"
"Why?"
"I don't want to die without you.
"You shall live forever."
"How can you be so sure?"

"You have an aura of wisdom, an aura of desire, and you're blessed with longevity."

"Are you giving me a reading? You're a woman of many talents, but I'm skeptical about this aura-thing, I just can't see it."

"Your aura is something you can't really see, but others around you can."

Time 18:00

"I owe you the world. For everything you gave me. I now believe that life has a meaning. I thought I hated women, because I hated my mother. Now, everything is different, Jenny, everything is crystal clear. Everything is?"

"Everything is fine, Mark; everything is fine. Your mother loves you. They all love you here in this house."

"And I love you. I do."

"And I love you too, but you must understand."

"No, I'm not allowed to understand, my heart won't let me."

"There's a new disease around the world."

"Speak to me, what is it?"

"Are you afraid of love?"

"I'm afraid to be terribly lonely."

"In this case a statue might be the answer."

"Your statue, the Ducati girl statue, I shall venerate it as a goddess, right in my bedroom, but I'm afraid a statue could mean the end of life."

"Tell me; what's my fault, to be here?"

Time 19:00

"I didn't know love before I spent these incredible afternoons with you. Everybody loves you, my friends can't stop talking about you and I can't sleep without thinking about you. What have you done to me?"

"What have I done to you, Sandra?"

"You were the very first one to talk about love. In a way, you have declared war to my soul."

"Uh, that must be frightening."

"It was at first, but now that I know you, I'm no longer afraid."

"All I probably did was showing you the road."

"And destiny, what is my destiny without you? What is love, another type of cancer without cure? Tell me."

"I must go."

"No, don't leave me behind!"

"I'll give you a cup of coffee."

"No, please, listen to me."

"You need to get dressed before your mother knocks on the door."

"Mother is in love with you."

"No."

"I saw you together yesterday, and the day before, and the day?"

"No, that was you."

"Together?"

"Together."

"Father, mother, brother, everybody is in love with you."

"Well, so conceited of you, I must say."

"Why?"
"That you only love yourself."
"I am not conceited."
"What's love to you?"
"Everything."
"Tell me what I don't know."
"I must go."
"I don't want to lose you."
"You take care of yourself."
"No, I want to take care of you."

Time 20:00

"You're more attractive than hope, but you made me miserable. What's going to happen to me?"

"I don't know."

"Why are we so afraid to live a life without worries? When I was a child, the major concern was freedom, now it's love. Because love is the cancer of the new generation and the stem cells are me, I, and myself. The very first love poem was written in Latin, a language that is dead, therefore love belongs to the dead. The love for material things is what I meant; it's developing agony. To have or not to have. A man cross dressed as a woman marries a man dressed as a man; it just happened yesterday, I saw it with my own eyes. I'm old fashioned, you must forgive me. Such is fear to man, fear to be lonely. My home is no longer home, it's a place of business, a place of negotiations, my own Davos, and now a confessional."

"Do you love me?"

"Look at my face."

"I've no interest in anything at this moment. I don't even have interest for my family anymore. There's never being so much emptiness in my life; but now that you're here, I have a reason to live again."

"I have a daunting task ahead of me."

"It was an empty road of false ideas. You have filled my life. But now that you're leaving me, you're destroying everything. I'm terribly afraid to lose you. I'm terribly afraid that I will fall ill again. You came as a messiah to destroy everything and now you can shout fait accompli."

"De rien. There isn't always a purpose in life. Have you seen Mela? I might need help."

"She left the house for good early in the morning. She took the camera with your pictures on it."

"Where is she?"

"Home, back with her parents. She left something for you, the soap bubble solution, her special recipe; she wants you to keep it with you in your Ducati."

"I will. Now I shall let you go back to your family affairs."

"No, it's too late. It's impossible to restore any credibility at this point."

"Nothing belongs to me; there wasn't any reason for such attempt in the first place. I wish I could wake up from this terrible nightmare. What I wanted was totally different, totally unique, totally real. I guess some people have absolutely no talent for making good choices. I took some shortcuts and this is what I've got. I wish I could start all over again, as a newborn, but I'm afraid I don't have much time left."

"Mark, you have plenty of time."

"No, the truth is the sad truth; I'm no earth, I'm no sun, I'm no sky, and I'm no moon; I'm terribly average, and hardly unique, I must no longer fool myself and the ones around me. Fire, water and air have a purpose and an idea on where to go; I do not."

"Well, I guess we're on the same boat."

Index

www.ingramcontent.com/pod-product-compliance
Lightning Source LLC
LaVergne TN
LVHW050314160826
845677LV00014B/3381
9798422223015